Spiced

Spiced

A Pastry Chef's True Stories of
Trials by Fire, After-Hours Exploits,
and What Really Goes on in the Kitchen

DALIA

JURGENSEN

G. P. PUTNAM'S SONS · NEW YORK

PUTNAM

G. P. PUTNAM'S SONS
Publishers Since 1838
Published by the Penguin Group
Penguin Group (USA) Inc., 375 Hudson Street, New York, New York 10014,
USA · Penguin Group (Canada), 90 Eglinton Avenue East, Suite 700, Toronto,
Ontario M4P 2Y3, Canada (a division of Pearson Canada Inc.) · Penguin Books Ltd,
80 Strand, London WC2R 0RL, England · Penguin Ireland, 25 St Stephen's
Green, Dublin 2, Ireland (a division of Penguin Books Ltd) · Penguin Group
(Australia), 250 Camberwell Road, Camberwell, Victoria 3124, Australia (a division
of Pearson Australia Group Pty Ltd) · Penguin Books India Pvt Ltd, 11 Community
Centre, Panchsheel Park, New Delhi–110 017, India · Penguin Group (NZ),
67 Apollo Drive, Rosedale, North Shore 0632, New Zealand (a division of Pearson
New Zealand Ltd) · Penguin Books (South Africa) (Pty) Ltd, 24 Sturdee Avenue,
Rosebank, Johannesburg 2196, South Africa

Penguin Books Ltd, Registered Offices: 80 Strand, London WC2R 0RL, England

Library of Congress Cataloging-in-Publication Data

Jurgensen, Dalia.
Spiced / Dalia Jurgensen.
p.   cm.
ISBN 978-0-399-15561-1
1. Jurgensen, Dalia.   2. Cooks—New York (State)—New York—Biography.
3. Pastry—New York (State)—New York.   I. Title.
TX649.J97A3   2009   2008046364
641.5092—dc22
[B]

Printed in the United States of America
1   3   5   7   9   10   8   6   4   2

BOOK DESIGN BY AMANDA DEWEY

For Matthew

Spiced is my story, and a work of nonfiction. But, in the interest of privacy, some names and identifying characteristics have been changed or simply left out. I've also taken the liberty of compressing time lines and moving a few events out of sequence in order to advance the story. However, all of the nicknames (with the exception of two) and all the other crazy stuff that happens, along with the outrageous things that are said, are absolutely true. Restaurants are full of nutty people who do nutty things, and that's why I love them.

Spiced

ONE

Getting into Nobu

"Order, fire!" screamed Steven from the window that sepa-rated the small, open kitchen from the dining room. He was the middleman, reducing the handwritten orders dropped off by hustling waiters to single key words or phrases—restaurant "shorthand"—that he yelled out to the cooks. Each urgent order spurred them into action, executing the seemingly endless array and combinations of plates. I watched Steven from my spot at the edge of the kitchen as he finished yelling out orders through the window, which also served as a clear dividing line between two worlds: the clean, well-dressed diners enjoying a relaxed meal beneath warm light on one side, the sweat-drenched cooks toiling under the shock of fluorescents to meet their demands on the other.

"Fire! Four *hamachi kama,* four new-style, three squid pasta, two *anticucho,* two kobe, and six—six *omakase saikyo!*"

Almost as though compensating for his short stature, Steven used every cell in his body to get his message across. The veins in his face bulged, and his short, fair hair seemed to stretch farther and farther away from his scalp with every subsequent order he yelled.

It was my first night "trailing" at Nobu, the hottest new restaurant in New York City's crowded and competitive restaurant scene. Trailing, I had learned, was part of the interviewing process in the restaurant world. I would have an opportunity to see what my potential workplace would be like, and Mika, Nobu's Japanese pastry chef, who had granted me the trail despite my utter lack of experience, would see firsthand if I fit into my new environment. I still had two weeks left at my day job as a sales and marketing coordinator at a publishing house, and the year-long weekend culinary program I had enrolled in didn't start for a week after that, but that night marked the start of a career I'd had in the back of my mind since I was a small child, and it was like magic.

I took it all in, every movement, every odor and sound, every single unfamiliar word and food. I studied the cooks, dressed in white double-breasted jackets and ultrabaggy pants designed with colorful underwater fish scenes, who sprang into action as soon as Steven's words burst into the hot air. They threw pans onto gas burners, seasoned fish, and sprinkled herbs, producing perfectly composed plates of food quickly and efficiently. I stared in awe at their rough grace. Through shouts of "Behind!" "Open oven!"

and "Pick up!" I felt the kitchen swell with the cooks' collective energy. The kitchen was alive. It breathed. It sweat.

A suited and suntanned man with an easy smile stuck his head past Steven and in through the kitchen's window. His neat, well-groomed figure was incongruous with the down-and-dirty vibe of the kitchen. He looked like one of the customers.

"Woody's on fifty-three with Soon-Yi," he notified everyone, causing only the faintest of ripples in the energy. The room acknowledged him with a slight nod, but its overall movement surged on without skipping a beat. "Let's make them happy!" he finished and was gone.

I turned to Mika, my teacher for the night. She had been showing me how to work the pastry station, patiently explaining how the kitchen functioned.

"He comes in all the time." She shrugged without dislodging a single black hair of her pin-straight bob, answering the question that my eyebrows had been asking. She continued to organize the many items on the pastry station, which consisted of two waist-high stainless steel refrigerators topped with a six-foot-by-one-foot length of white removable countertop that doubled as a cutting board. The area just behind the cutting board was hollowed out so that a multitude of smaller rectangular stainless steel containers of various sizes could be nestled into the top of the refrigerators and remain cold throughout the evening. The wall above was lined with two thick stainless steel shelves (stainless steel, the material of choice in the kitchen, gave it an endless number of reflective metallic surfaces) that held various containers of cookies, stacks of plates, and other items whose purpose I didn't yet understand.

Mika assured me that dessert orders would soon be pouring in and that we would be very busy. She had no time for celebrity sightings. I, on the other hand, was duly impressed. Woody Allen! My night was just getting better and better. Any second thoughts I'd had about rashly quitting my dull office job a few weeks earlier quickly melted away. In the few hours I'd spent in Nobu's kitchen, my eyes had feasted on more energy and life than in the entire two and a half years I'd spent in my previous job. As far as I could tell, the only priority in the kitchen was to successfully prepare food ordered by the customers. It was task oriented, devoid of any need for sales reports, signature approvals, disingenuous small talk, or distasteful brownnosing. The food had to be prepared with quality, speed, and integrity. It was honest and pure. It was perfect. And I wanted to be a part of it.

I began to feel more at ease in my starched white chef's jacket. As the dessert orders began to trickle in, Mika methodically showed me how to execute every one, stressing the importance of detail. I concentrated on everything she told me.

"Every plate must be exactly the same," she said softly with a lilting Japanese accent, her full, round face nodding with every movement. She placed slices of chocolate *maki* (a chocolate cake filled with ginger mousse that was rolled up and coated in toasted almond flour to mimic a sushi roll) on a black lacquer rectangle. She carefully filled a tiny white bowl with bright orange passion fruit sauce and placed it beside the *maki* slices. Finally, she slid a pair of chocolate chopsticks flecked with edible gold leaf into a paper sleeve that was printed with the Nobu logo and laid it across the *maki*. With that, the dessert was ready for the customer.

Mika presented each dessert in this same way, patiently explaining which plate to start out with (plain, white round or heavy, tan-speckled earthenware or shiny black lacquer) and then detailed each component of the dessert and its position on the plate. Soon, though, the area around me became a flurry of small white paper slips, and Mika was forced to switch from teacher mode to super fast production mode. Calm and soothing before, Mika now became a machine. She worked quickly and deftly, treating each component with respect, creating plate after plate of wondrous dessert: chocolate *maki,* ginger crème brûlée, Asian pear granita, and some things, like *mochi* ice cream (a small ball of ice cream wrapped in gummy rice flour dough) and *ogura* (a sweet red bean paste), I'd never seen before. I watched her, trying to keep them all straight in my head, worrying that she might test me later. Soon the orders were coming in even faster. Impossibly, Mika's speed increased as she moved with a silent fury to complete them.

I stood by feeling helpless, still lacking the skill or knowledge to assist her. I stared at the tickets lined up on the shelf in front of Mika and tried to decipher the many words, some of them profoundly unfamiliar, until I spotted an order for green tea ice cream. Ice cream! I remembered that plate; it was one of the simpler ones. Plus, I had worked in ice cream stores for six years through high school and college, and if there was one thing I *did* have confidence in, it was my ability to scoop. I grabbed a cold plate from the refrigerator under me and reached for the oval-shaped scoop that sat in a small bin of constantly running water. In a matter of seconds, I'd arranged three ovals—quenelles, Mika had called them—of green tea ice cream on the thick earthenware plate the way she had shown me earlier. I paused, looking at the plate. Something was missing; it was too plain. Without looking up, Mika pointed her nose toward a plastic container of cookies labeled ALMOND TUILES. Right! Almond tuiles. I placed one of the thin, flat, curved, diamond-shaped cookies on top of the ice cream and handed it, along with the ticket that held the corresponding table information, to a passing waiter.

"Pick up?" I asked him. "Please?"

The waiter paused, noticing me, a strange new face in the kitchen, for the first time. After a moment of consideration, he took the ice cream off my hands, dropped the ticket into the trash, and delivered it to the correct table. Mission accomplished. I did it! I turned back to the line of tickets, looking for more ice cream orders. I scooped my little heart out, filling any ice cream and sorbet orders that came in, and handing them off to any waiter that happened to pass by. When there was nothing to be scooped, I used the small boost in my confidence to help Mika in other ways, like filling tiny bowls with passion fruit sauce, tending only to the small details I remembered for certain, those I knew I had no chance of screwing up.

Finally, the tide of white tickets began to ebb. With only a few left on the shelf, I took a breath and noticed that the order for table fifty-three was among the remaining tickets. It listed no desserts and was instead labeled only with the letters VIP. I looked over at Mika, who was preparing a beautiful assortment of desserts on a large white platter. The platter was almost full, with only a single corner left unfilled. Mika looked up at me for the first time in over an hour and handed me a ginger crème brûlée.

"You want to make it?" she asked, smiling at me knowingly. I grabbed the stainless steel shaker of sugar and waved it back and forth over the brûlée, coating the top with a thin, even layer of sugar. I wiped the edge of the ramekin with my index finger to remove any excess sugar, the way Mika had shown me earlier, to prevent any sugar from burning on the ramekin's white edge, which would make it look sloppy. She nodded approvingly and handed me the tank of propane. With a click of my finger, the torch switched on, and its blue flame came blistering out. It felt serious and a little bit dangerous. Trying to keep my trepidation hidden, I tentatively moved the flaming wand evenly over the sugar, gradually transforming the layer of white grains into a bubbling, deep brown sheet of caramel. I turned off the torch and looked hopefully at Mika.

"Perfect," she said, placing the crème brûlée on the platter's empty corner. "It's ready."

She stood in the kitchen doorway and grabbed the first waiter she saw, forcibly recruiting him to deliver the VIP dessert. Then she turned back to me.

"You can see him if you stand next to the espresso machine," Mika said, waving me toward her. "Watch where the waiter goes."

I took my position and, with my eyes, followed the waiter to the back of the dining room. Waiters and busboys continued to file in and out of the kitchen, but I kept my eyes on that tray of desserts as it traveled through the dining room until it landed on the table where Woody Allen, Soon-Yi, and their tablemates would share the ginger crème brûlée whose edge I had wiped clean with my virgin finger. From where I stood I could just barely catch a glimpse of a silver spoon digging into the dessert, cracking its deep caramel crust, and revealing the silky custard beneath.

I returned to Mika's side at the dessert station, where she was wiping down the counter and restoring order after the insanity of the night's dessert rush. She explained that there were no slow nights at Nobu, which had a minimum of 275 reservations for dinner every night, stressing that what I had experienced that night was the norm and that if I worked there I would have to be able to handle it—every night.

"What do you think?" she asked me.

"I like it," I answered. It was an understatement, but I didn't want to gush and risk sounding silly or worse, like I wasn't taking it seriously. I liked the energy, creating the plates of desserts and knowing that when they arrived at a table, people's faces might light up. The kitchen had been filled with so many unfamiliar things, but at the same time, it felt natural to me. I wanted to be part of it, wearing the baggy fish pants like everyone else, serving up food every night.

"I mean," I added, "I would like to work here." I had to make it clear.

"Okay." She smiled. "I'll talk to Jemal."

Jemal was the other pastry chef, whom I hadn't met yet, and was obviously someone else whose standards I'd have to meet before being offered a job.

I stayed until the last dessert order was filled and the station thoroughly cleaned and organized in preparation for lunch the next day. I then returned to the dank, narrow hallway in the basement where I'd left my street clothes hanging on a peg, not far from a tub of Japanese pickles fermenting in the corner. After changing, I dropped my chef's coat into a bin of dirty clothes, stuffed my pants into my backpack, and, after thanking Mika for the night, walked out through the dining room, where a few straggling customers were lingering over the last of their sake or one more mug of green tea, empty dessert plates still in front of some of them. *I helped make that,* I wanted to tell them proudly. Though it was after midnight, I briskly walked the fifteen minutes to my train, high from my first night in a restaurant kitchen.

✦

TWO

Seeds of Inspiration

I had always wanted to be a chef. Even still, I had not planned on spontaneously quitting my publishing job that day, a week before I'd even heard about the possibility of trailing at Nobu. I'd enrolled in culinary school a month earlier, but it was a weekend program only, and I'd planned on staying at my office job while in school. Once I'd taken that step into the restaurant world, though, my job began feeling less and less important, even if it did provide a steady paycheck and health insurance. With cooking now firmly in my future, I was eager to escape the small office where I spent my hours staring alternately at the glare of my computer screen and out through my window at the city below. The pile of uncomfortable work shoes I'd stashed beneath my desk (I had no need for them outside of the office) depressed me. They seemed to serve no valuable purpose.

My parents were generally supportive of my decision. Maybe it was their Danish background: They had different and more flexible ideas about career and education, and they saw nothing inherently wrong with my decision to drastically switch careers— my Danish cousins did it all the time. They made no case in favor of the "security" of an office job with a large company. Neither one had exactly followed an orthodox career path. My mother started college at thirty-four and eventually became a computer programmer after being a stay-at-home mom. And my father left home at thirteen after being given an ultimatum by his mother: Go to school or get a job. He went to sea, became a sea captain, and did not retire until he was sixty-six years old. It was my father who ultimately encouraged my step away from office life for good.

"Dad," I lamented on the phone one day from work, "I just don't feel like any of this stuff matters. The reports, the trade shows, the promotional materials. People only care about bottom lines. It's not *interesting*. It's not me. I feel stifled."

"I'll tell you one thing I know for sure," he'd said. "You only have one life. Whatever you decide to do, you should try and be happy. Don't be afraid to take risks."

And that's all it took. I hung up the phone and immediately gave my two weeks' notice. I figured I'd find a job waiting tables for the next nine months while in culinary school. At least I'd be in a restaurant and not staring at a computer.

A week later, I heard about the job opening at Nobu through

Linda, a friend of a friend. When she revealed that she was a cook at Nobu, I excitedly told her about culinary school, my recent decision to quit publishing, and my plan to wait tables. Linda told me that Nobu was looking for a nighttime pastry person, an entry-level position. "You should check it out," she said. It had to be kismet.

A few days later I met with Mika, and I liked her immediately. I was encouraged by her kind tone.

"I've wanted to cook for as long as I can remember," I told her, banking on my enthusiasm, my only credential.

It was the absolute truth. I have always loved to cook. At five, I stood on a chair at the counter next to my mother and helped her with the many Danish dishes she prepared, shaping *frikadeller,* peeling potatoes for *bikser mad.* For dessert, she showed me how to sprinkle bread crumbs, toasted with butter to a deep brown, in a fat layer over the apples she'd cooked down the night before. I watched intently as she magically whipped cream into a fluffy cloud and used it for another layer of the *æblecage.* And when she made bread, I waited anxiously for the ball of dough resting in a glass bowl on the stovetop to puff up until finally it would be time for my tiny fist to punch down the plump, airy pillow. Then she would knead it again, shaping most of it into two loaves and giving me my own bit of dough to shape in any way I wanted: a short braid, a pretzel, a turtle. And when the bread was done baking (my small shapes were always done first) we gobbled it down as soon as it was cool enough to handle, slathering it with plenty of butter and sometimes a sprinkle of brown sugar. For my thirteenth birthday, I received Anne Willan's *Grand Diplôme Cooking Course* cookbook as a gift and read it over and over. Mesmerized by the photos, I attempted some of the less complicated recipes. After graduating high school, I still wanted to cook, but I was interested in so many other things, too. I wanted to study languages and literature, so I went to a conventional university. I kept cooking, but only as a hobby.

"I spend all my spare time baking and cooking at home," I told Mika. I still routinely pored over cookbooks, using my roommates and boyfriend as guinea pigs for elaborate dinners and brunches.

Sitting across from Mika that day, I felt overdressed in the pale yellow linen pantsuit I'd worn to work that day—like an imposter. Mika seemed so at ease in her baggy white chef's coat. I made sure to tell her that I was starting culinary school in just a few weeks. As luck would have it, I had enrolled in the very same school that Mika had attended.

On my second trail, I worked with Nobu's other pastry chef, Jemal, in the hours preceding dinner service. Jemal was a good foot taller than Mika (and me) and not nearly as soothing. He gave me orders and corrected my mistakes—all business. We worked down in the basement, where all the preparation for the upstairs service kitchen was done. He gave me simple tasks like peeling Asian pears (much rounder and crunchier than regular pears, with a texture like that of jicama), picking mint sprigs for garnish, and weighing ingredients. He said we were doing *mise-*

en-place, getting all the ingredients together. Every task, every dessert, it seemed, had its own set of *mise-en-place.*

After a few hours of work, Jemal led me outside the restaurant, where we sat on the ledge of an old loading dock.

"Your main responsibility if you work here," he told me, "will be plating desserts—like what you did the other night with Mika. You'd also be responsible for setting up the *mise-en-place* for the station—all the little things, garnishes and stuff. In addition to that," he went on, "you'd be doing some light production—simple cakes, phyllo cups, things like that. We'll teach you that stuff."

So far, neither Mika nor Jemal seemed to mind that I had no experience and hadn't even started school yet. They didn't even seem to mind that I had enrolled in a culinary program that did not include pastry. The program at school that combined savory and pastry was too expensive, and I'd been forced to choose. I chose savory, thinking I'd be better at it.

"Your lack of experience doesn't bother me," he said finally. "It just means that I can mold you any way I want. That you haven't learned any bad habits yet." He smiled, almost maniacally. I just nodded. I wanted him to teach me everything, especially since I wouldn't be learning it at school. It was the perfect situation.

"So," he finally said, "the job pays four hundred dollars a week—that's before taxes—and you'll work Monday through Friday starting at two p.m. every day. You'll work until the last dessert has gone out and the station is cleaned and closed down, which will rarely be before midnight. I want you to know exactly what you're getting yourself into." He paused while I took it all in. I couldn't believe it. I was actually being offered a job, a *cooking* job, in a real restaurant. And not just any old restaurant but a great one. One in the spotlight.

"You know," he finally added, almost grudgingly, "Mika really likes you. We're willing to give you a chance."

✥

THREE

Melting Point

I abruptly stopped cutting my pineapple, crossed my fingers, and headed toward the oven.

"Behind you!"

From my position at the pastry station, which sat perpendicular to the end of the hot line, I declared my intention to enter the area of Nobu's kitchen that was lined with dangerously fiery ovens, broilers, fryers, and stovetop steamers on one side; refrigeration, cutting boards, and countertops on the other; and four cooks, elbow to elbow, down the narrow middle corridor, one per station, mediating and mastering their respective areas. During lunch and dinner service, the line was the belly of the kitchen beast, a fury of activity bulging with dervish-like cooks, flying sauté pans, and food in various stages of preparation. But dinner service was still more than an hour away, and the line was in a state of relative calm as the cooks readied their stations for the impending battle: 298 reservations that night. I'd been a full-time, paid employee of the restaurant for more than five weeks, but I was still intimidated by the line: its power, its muscle, its cloud of testosterone. Its sheer foreignness. I hated going there, but the only oven in the restaurant sat midway down its path, and I had to check my génoise, the sponge cake we used for the chocolate *maki*.

"Behind you!" I announced again, edging down the line as the cooks responded to my voice by leaning over their counters in order to let me by.

"Behind you!" I went on, trying to increase the volume of my voice. *You have to speak loud!* Yuki, an older Japanese cook, had said. *People have to know where you are, when you are coming, what to expect! Maybe someone gonna bump into you! If you don't tell them, maybe you gonna get burned!* Yuki was the de facto leader of the hot line, and he scared me.

I had yet to suffer any physical injury, but the heads shaking in disappointed disgust and the harsh looks I'd received—especially from the sushi chefs, the stern, quiet commanders of the kitchen—had been injury enough. Speaking loudly and often did not come naturally to me, but then again, getting fired and allowing a golden opportunity to slip through my fingers wouldn't feel very good, either. I tried my best.

"Open oven!" I continued loudly, lowering the heavy bottom-hinged door of the hulking oven that, when open, almost fully blocked the path of the line, dividing it in two.

I grabbed the first of the two wide, flat sheets of chocolate génoise from the oven, holding each side with a folded kitchen towel to protect my hands from the hot metal. Resting the sheet on the stovetop, I futilely checked the cakes for doneness, more for show than anything else. The génoise barely resisted the gentle press of my finger, confirming what the cake's darkened edges (and my earlier panic) had already told me: I had overbaked the chocolate génoise. Again.

Quietly swallowing my disappointment and hoping that the cooks would not notice my failure, I pulled the other sheet from the oven and set it on top of the first slightly askew so that I could carry them both down to the basement to cool in the pastry prep area.

"Hot!" I yelled, balancing the large sheets of cake on one flat, upturned hand over my right shoulder, using my left hand to steady the edges. "Coming through!"

"Hot!" I insisted every few steps.

"*Caliente!*" I barked in Spanish, one of the kitchen's other languages, trying to keep my volume up, ignoring the inevitable response of *"Como yo!"* that came from someone in my path.

"Funny," I said back. My usual response. I had yet to come up with a better comeback. Revealing any irritation or indignation, I knew, would only encourage or, worse, amuse.

"Hot behind!" I continued on my way.

"I'll say!" came the answer. It was an exasperating, losing battle, and I hadn't gone more than a few yards.

I turned the corner past the pot-washing station, taking a deep breath as I started down the precariously narrow stairway that felt to me, with two hot sheet pans awkwardly balanced over one shoulder, more like a death trap: the final obstacle before having to announce my failure to the two pastry chefs who had, in a moment of probable desperation, hired my wholly inexperienced ass. Whatever honeymoon period I'd enjoyed those first few exciting days was soon overshadowed by my ineptitude. What I *did* quickly learn was that nothing was easy in my new world, a world into which I'd so eagerly and happily jumped. Something as simple as walking through the kitchen required a specific vocabulary and a new attitude. And that was just the beginning.

I didn't just make cakes anymore; I made génoise. To do this, I separated eggs and whipped the yolks with sugar until they reached *ribbon stage*. I sifted *AP* flour (not to be confused with bread or pastry flour) with cocoa powder before folding it into the yolk mixture. Virtually everything was weighed in grams, not measured in cups or teaspoons. After dividing the finished génoise batter between two parchment-lined sheet pans, I smoothed it as evenly as I could, given my rudimentary skill level, with an *offset spatula*. Finally, I baked the cakes. For how long? And this is where things really got tricky. *Until they were done.* That's what Jemal said. *Use your internal clock.* Timers, I found out, were frowned upon as crutches used only by home cooks—loser amateurs in the outside world. Meanwhile, my own internal clock was in some serious need of calibration, as was the quickly eroding state of my ego.

"Coming through!"

I descended the stairs into the basement, a small crowded factory of preparatory movement. The sushi chefs dominated the basement until service started, at which point they had to take their places in the dining room behind the sushi bar. Until then, they lined up at long cutting boards stretched across deep stainless steel sinks, where they swiftly inspected and butchered fish and pummeled open par-cooked lobsters in order to remove their tender flesh, which, much to Jemal's dismay, inevitably led to an indiscriminate spraying of milky lobster juice around the prep area. They sharpened their expensive knives often, sliding them swiftly back and forth across a small rectangle of a two-toned stone, *swish-swash . . . swish-swash . . . swish-swash.* For the most part, the sushi chefs kept to themselves, pausing in their private conversations only to bark out orders at Kim, the sushi *commis,* a low-level apprentice, who seemed to me more of a whipping boy. He did any and all of the sushi chefs' dirty work, waiting for the day he would be deemed "ready" even to touch the fish, let alone begin learning the precision cuts. Clearly miserable, Kim was usually downright unpleasant with me. I got the feeling that his one joy in life was having someone in the kitchen who was lower down the totem pole than he was. When he did, on occasion, offer a rare friendly word, I was suspicious. As for the rest of the sushi chefs, they hardly ever acknowledged me with anything more than a sniff.

"Hot!"

Jemal and Mika looked up as I made my way toward them. I was still trying to figure out the hierarchy of our small pastry department. Both Jemal's and Mika's names were printed at the bottom of the dessert menu and both held the title of pastry chef, but I was confused about who was ultimately in charge. Jemal certainly assumed that position, with his air of confidence and absolute opinions, and it had been he, not Mika, who had officially offered me the job. But Mika had all the knowledge of traditional Japanese desserts, and it was she to whom the waiters, and sometimes even the sushi chefs, turned when they wanted to treat special customers to dessert, especially Japanese customers. I didn't want to risk embarrassment or offend either one by making any assumptions, and there wasn't anyone else I could ask. Linda, the woman through whom I had initially gotten the interview with Mika, still worked at Nobu, but she had little time for me now. It turned out that the job opening that she had told me about, the job I currently held, was actually her *old* job. She'd been cooking for years, a veteran of high-end restaurants like the River Café in Brooklyn, and had taken the lowly entry-level job of pastry cook just to get her foot in Nobu's enviable door. The only way she could move onto the hot line, where she really wanted to be, was to find someone to take her position. Once my arrival facilitated that, she became focused on proving herself in the all-male kitchen and quickly began to make her mark. The few pointers she gave me were sporadic and, at the time, cryptic: *Always stir a cooling pot . . . anticipate your chef's next step . . . it's all about timing.* She might as well have been speaking Swahili. I navigated the hierarchy of the pastry department on my own.

Mika and Jemal were aesthetic opposites. Mika, Japanese and diminutive, was quiet and calculated in her movements and had a voice that cooed, never betraying even a tiny trace of arrogance. Jemal, on the other hand, multiply pierced and tattooed, towered above both of us and had a booming voice that he was not shy about using, despite frowns from the more reserved Japanese chefs in the kitchen, who kept their chatter to a minimum while prepping in the basement. He had a flop of hair that alternated between electric blue, platinum, and clown red. Before Nobu, the chef/owner of the eponymous restaurant, offered Jemal the job of pastry chef, he had had one final question: *But why do you do this to your hair, your ears?* Jemal was resolute and unapologetic with his answer: *I'm a creative person.* Despite having such diametrically opposed personalities, Mika and Jemal had an identical response to my overbaked génoise: an exasperated sigh. *What are we going to do with her?*

"Just put them on the rack," said Jemal dismissively.

"I'm sorry," I said, sliding the sheets onto the short cooling rack in the corner of the pastry area. What else could I say?

"Should I make another batch?" I offered. Jemal glanced at his watch.

"Just do the *mise-en-place*," he said. "We have enough *maki* for tonight."

"I'll make it tomorrow," offered Mika, inspecting my overdone cakes to see if they could be salvaged at all, maybe reincarnated as miniature rum balls as she'd done before. It was a small consolation.

"Is my chocolate melted yet?" asked Jemal, not looking up from the plastic stencil he was creating using an X-Acto knife and the top to a tub of sour cream.

Oh no. My eyes widened. The chocolate!

"I'll check," I said, trying to hide my panic. I had completely and utterly forgotten about the chocolate he'd asked me to melt.

I was supposed to stir it often, making sure the heat remained low. Pastry items left unattended on the stove among the cooks' many pots had the potential to get messed up, I'd been warned. *Cooks don't care about pastry. They don't appreciate what we do.* How long had it been? I cursed my faulty internal clock.

"Behind!" I yelled as I raced upstairs, back to the inside of the line. The dark chocolate was right where I'd left it: melting in a stainless steel bowl, resting on top of a large pot that had a few fingers of water in it . . . over high heat. *Always melt chocolate gently, over low heat,* Jemal had said. *Getting it too hot changes the way it tastes, the way it acts.* I was supposed to lower the heat to a slight simmer as soon as the water came up to a boil and then periodically check on it. How long ago was that?

I flicked off the burner. Using side towels, I grabbed the large bowl of chocolate and noticed that the edges of the chocolate looked dry and crusted over.

Oh no.

With horror, I noticed that the pot underneath was completely out of water and must have been for some time. For so long, in fact, that a tiny hole—an actual hole!—had been burned through its blackened and ashy bottom. I was in a stupor, holding the bowl of chocolate. This was worse than overbaking the génoise. Much worse.

"Oh . . . my . . . God!" said Herman, a line cook, looking over my shoulder and into the pot. He lingered over each word, accentuating his disbelief. He bit his lower lip and sucked in a long breath. I just stared at the pot.

"You made a hole?" asked another incredulously. I nodded. I had. I had made a hole. I really had. Not only had I burned the chocolate (failed task number two of the day), but I had actually burned it so successfully, forgotten about it so completely, that I had etched an actual hole in a metal pot.

I carried the bowl of chocolate to the pastry station at the end of the line, then went back to the pot where the rest of the cooks had gathered to witness the seemingly impossible.

"It's ruined," someone said, stating the obvious. Someone else whistled in disbelief. It was as if all the cooks, who until that point had tolerated the new girl, the girl with no experience who had to be taught everything, even how to speak up, were suddenly saying *We knew it.* I was frozen with humiliation. I was a tiny speck of dust on the filthy kitchen floor, where discarded scraps got swept aside and stepped on. Worse, I was going to be fired.

Not all my days had been that bad. Sure, I made lots of mistakes, most of them small, like forgetting to chiffonade the *shiso* leaf, one of the garnishes for the pastry station, or not slicing the Asian pears uniformly. Mika and Jemal had been patient, assuring me that with time, practice, and repetition I would be unable *not* to improve. And I *was* pretty good at doing service, quickly composing plates of already completed pastry items for anxious diners. My fruit plates still needed a fair amount of work, as did my chocolate writing, but by then, I was yelling at waiters—some of them by name, even—*and* getting them to pick up their orders. I still had some trouble with the more advanced production tasks (obviously) and with timing. But burning a hole through a pot?

This might cancel out whatever minute strides I'd made. The dangerously thin ice I'd been on that day might have just cracked.

Mika appeared upstairs, noticed the circle of activity around the pot, and came to inspect the scene.

"You made a *hole*?" she said, looking at the pot, eyebrows raised in disbelief. Her accent made it sometimes difficult to discern the meaning of her tone. Was she amused? Accusing? Infuriated? I braced myself and nodded, waiting for the inevitable: my invitation to the door.

But then she began to laugh. She grabbed the pot with a side towel, brought it to the pot sink, and ran cold water over it before dropping it into the trash. She giggled quietly, shoulders shaking the entire time.

"I'll pay for it," I said sheepishly, finally looking her in the eye. She shook her head and let out a full laugh.

"You know," she said smilingly, ignoring my offer, "everybody does something."

I wasn't sure how to respond. I certainly *had* done something.

"When they start," she explained. "Everybody does *something*. Makes some mistake."

I just stared at her.

"It's okay," she assured me. She looked at her watch. "You finish setting up the station for service." She set her hand on my shoulder. "I'll tell Jemal. Don't worry." She took the bowl of ruined chocolate downstairs.

Still wary of the security of my position in the restaurant but thankful, so thankful, for the encouraging and ever-supportive Mika, I returned to the pastry station, which contained nothing I could burn or overcook. I finished cutting the pineapple I'd left sitting in a juicy pool, then picked through a bouquet of mint, plucking out the small, perfect sprigs for garnish—two tasks I could perform with relative confidence.

Even though I was the lowest member of the kitchen staff and felt like a complete failure, I reminded myself that I was working, unbelievable as it seemed, in one of New York City's best restaurants. Even the really bad days, and they couldn't possibly get any worse than today, were worth all the humiliation and failure.

Once the station was set up completely and I'd triple-checked everything, I made a small cornet out of parchment paper and filled it with melted chocolate. After folding over the top edges of the paper cone to seal its wide opening, I snipped a small hole at the bottom and spent the next fifteen minutes practicing my chocolate writing so that I'd be able to write "Happy Birthday" and other messages that customers sometimes requested with their desserts. Holding the cornet about an inch above a sheet of parchment, I tried to apply even pressure as I wrote the alphabet in cursive as a single continuous word: *abcdefghijklmnopqrstuvwxyz.* I needed to get used to the feel of the chocolate, the way it flowed and responded to the movement of my hand—the key to good chocolate writing, according to Jemal. *Repetition breeds improvement.* Over and over I practiced, waiting for the small printer on my station to spit out dessert orders.

It was Friday, and I looked forward to a two-day break, determined to return on Monday revitalized, more focused, more capable. I looked forward, as well, to my weekend at culinary school, where, after only a month, I had been comforted to find that I was one of the better students in the class and one of the very few working in a high-end restaurant, already gaining real experience. It was a small consolation.

✦

FOUR

Course Work

After nearly a lifetime of wanting to become a chef, I'd like to say that I spent weeks researching all the different New York City culinary schools, comparing programs, checking the instructors' pedigrees, evaluating their job placement programs. But I didn't. I simply called the number I saw on a television commercial that emphasized career change and made an appointment with the New York Restaurant School. After acing a ridiculously easy basic math skills test, all I had to do was fill out some student loan forms, sign some papers, and I was in.

The majority of my fellow students were also career changers, though most were younger than me. Most were men, and at least one was rumored to have been recently incarcerated and to have enrolled in the school as part of a job rehabilitation program.

Some students had worked in kitchens, mostly in hotels or catering halls, and came to school with the hopes of improving their skills or at least gaining a leg up via a diploma. The majority of these students (predominantly the men) thought they knew more than the rest of us and were eager to show off their superiority. I kept my job at Nobu to myself for quite a while, not wanting to risk sounding arrogant. I'd already learned that working in a restaurant, even a highly regarded one, didn't necessarily mean you knew what you were doing.

Our classroom was set up to mimic a restaurant kitchen, with four stations, each with a set of burners, an oven, an overhead broiler, a grill, and a fryer. We sat attentively at four long stainless steel tables, each one of us in identical standard issue black-and-white-checked pants, starched chef's coat with our name, thick-soled black work shoes, and white socks. It was mandatory that we wear toques, the tall pleated paper hat that, to my mind, served no purpose but to get in the way. At Nobu, however, the cooks wore baseball caps or even just kerchiefs wrapped around their heads. We pastry people simply tied our hair back.

"You have chosen a difficult career," Chef Fenton, our teacher, greeted us on our first day. He was short, with a protruding belly and thinning hair, and bore a profound resemblance to Homer Simpson. He shuffled around the classroom, dressed like us but with black pants instead of our black-and-white-checked. He made it clear that the nine-month, part-time course in which we had enrolled was meant for serious students working toward a career in the culinary arts, not for weekend hobbyists, and we would be treated accordingly.

"If you think you're going to get out of school and make a lot of money, you are wrong." He paused, waiting for disappointment. We just sat there. "You will work fifty, sixty, seventy, sometimes eighty hours a week and be on your feet the entire time. You will do the same thing every day. The. Same. Thing. Every. Day. You *will* be yelled at."

Pause.

"If you do not love cooking—absolutely love it—then you should leave now while you can still get most of your money back, because there is no other reason to go into this business. No. Other. Reason."

Some people shifted on their stools; others stared back at him blankly. I waited, eager to move on to the actual learning part: the cooking. Enough with the intimidation.

He gave each of us a thick, black vinyl roll filled with tools: an eight-inch chef's knife, a three-inch paring knife, a boning knife, a tourneau knife, a whisk, wooden spoon, slotted spoon, rubber spatula, a set of measuring cups and spoons, and an eight-ounce ladle.

We had to learn about our tools before we could use them. We spent hours just on the knives: stainless steel versus carbon versus a hybrid, the virtues of a full tang (the metal of the blade extends into the full length of the handle, making it stronger), boning versus serrated versus tourneau (one with a short, curved blade ideal for "turning" vegetables, shaping them into small football shapes). I took notes as Chef Fenton went methodically through the rest of the tool kit, smirking when he got to the large kitchen spoons. He told us that slotted and nonslotted spoons were sometimes called female and male. *It's easy to remember,* he explained; *the female ones have the holes.*

Did he just say that? I looked around for someone to commiserate with. A couple of the younger guys snickered knowingly at his little joke. Was he kidding? Or just preparing us for the rumored sexism of kitchens? Marina, my only real friend in the class, an African-American woman fifteen years older than me, rolled her eyes in commiseration. We thought he was ridiculous.

We got used to his inappropriate remarks. They were easy to ignore, and coming from Homer Simpson, they hardly threatened us. When Chef Fenton failed to appear one day and was subsequently replaced by a series of rotating teachers, we simply assumed he'd finally offended the wrong person.

Once familiar with our tools, we were allowed to use them and spent an inordinate amount of time on knife skills: how quickly and effectively we could use our new knives to chop, cut, slice. We *brunoised* (chopped into tiny 2-millimeter squares) carrots; we *diced* (cut into ⅛- to ½-inch squares) potatoes; and we *chiffonaded* (sliced into very thin strips) leafy herbs, making sure the entire time that we remembered all the new vocabulary as well as how to perform the skills they referred to because both would appear on our test. If we practiced, we were promised, our muscles would eventually "remember" how to get the vegetables and herbs to cooperate.

Once we'd gotten the basics down, we did eventually move on to actual cooking, though with only nine months of weekend classes, we had to breeze through the culinary canon: a single day each was allotted to sautéing, frying, broiling, and roasting of meats; two to sauces; two to butchering (we did fish and shellfish one day, meat and poultry the next); a day to pasta; a day to Chinese cooking (I could have learned more going out to eat in nearby Chinatown); and so on until we were done. Though the classes were always hands-on, and our tests were practical exams in which we had to reproduce particular food items (pesto, a medium-rare burger, shrimp bisque), they were overviews nonetheless, and little of the actual information I'd been so intent on learning there really sank in.

Despite the brevity with which we covered each topic, I loved class. I loved learning the techniques behind the endless cookbooks I'd pored over since childhood, and I loved impressing my roommates, friends, and family with my ability. I had my job at Nobu to keep me grounded. I knew with absolute certainty that, contrary to what some culinary students believe (especially those who go through prestigious two-year culinary programs), culinary school is simply a step on the way to becoming a chef. No one, absolutely no one, walks out of school ready to be a chef. Cooking as a trade simply involves too densely packed a skill set to be picked up over a few months (or even years) within the walls of a protective classroom. Experience—real experience—is everything.

FIVE

Extra Virgin

For months after starting at Nobu, I was so consumed with the work details of my new job (and with school on the weekends) that I didn't—couldn't—consider the consequences my new job would have on my social life. Slowly, though, as I became better versed in my daily responsibilities and my new environment, I came up for air and began to notice the toll it was taking. I hadn't seen my roommates (and two closest friends) forever. We began to communicate via scribbled notes. *Phone bill due . . . Drinks on Sunday . . . Drinks ever?* By the time I got home from work, they were both in bed, and when I woke up late the next morning, they were long gone. Nearly every single friend from my former life (as I was beginning to think of it) was in the same nine-to-five boat. I feared I was destined to a personal life consisting of solo breakfasts and lonely late-night subway rides. I realized that if I was going to have any social life at all, I needed to fully embrace my new hours, my new coworkers, my new lifestyle.

After I'd been at Nobu just over two months, we received a three-star review from the *New York Times*. I didn't yet understand the enormous importance of such an event and what exactly it meant for the restaurant, but the accolade was cause for great celebration and many congratulations. Every employee received a letter of thanks for his or her contribution to the success of the restaurant (my contribution!), and our sister restaurant hosted a post-shift party in our honor.

The party was my first chance to socialize with my coworkers away from the ticking printer. Outside of the nervous, urgent energy of the kitchen, the waiters became individual people rather than anonymous waiter drones, and they, in turn, discovered that I actually knew words other than *pick* and *up*. Even the cooks relaxed a little and treated me less like an annoying little sister they had to keep an eye on and more like just another member of the kitchen. I happily joined the party, clinking glasses, downing beer, making small talk. I was finally experiencing my first taste of a long-standing restaurant world tradition: the after-work drink.

After that party, the cooks lost their icy edge but remained uninterested in relaxing with me over a drink after work. And who could blame them? They worked doubles and had to be back at work the following morning by ten a.m. But the waiters were a different story, and waiters, in all honesty, were much more interesting to hang out with. They were, after all, mostly artists, writers, dancers, or actors, and much more like my other friends than the cooks. The waiters were almost always up for a drink or a late-night snack. And in New York City, the city that never sleeps, there was no shortage of bars or restaurants to accommodate us.

Like most of the waitstaff at Nobu, Kelly was Japanese. Early on, I knew her only as one more waiter whizzing through the kitchen, dropping off dirty dishes, and picking up freshly plated desserts. Over time, though, as my comfort level at Nobu grew, so did my friendships. Kelly gradually became part of my small circle of friends, and we often ended up in the same place for drinks or late-night meals. She'd given herself an American name (for simplicity's sake, I guess) that was easier to remember than the rest of what were to me very exotic names. Her first choice had been Kiki, but someone else had told her it sounded too much like the name of a stripper.

After a while, our mutual friend, Misa, began dropping hints that Kelly liked me, which was great, since I liked her, too; she was easy to be with and eternally welcoming. But the hints continued, and Misa started relaying cryptic messages, even when Kelly was sitting right next to me: *She hopes this candy will be like a magic,* she said suggestively to me one late night after we'd just stuffed ourselves at a twenty-four-hour restaurant in Chinatown. Then she handed me a small candy that Kelly had given her. The two of them sat there smiling at me and then said something in Japanese. Magic? Magic love candy? I never knew if I was completely understanding correctly, or if something was getting lost in translation. I felt uncomfortable about coming right out and asking Kelly if she was flirting with me; I just ate the candy.

It wasn't a complete surprise to find Kelly still in the dining room when I returned upstairs in my street clothes after finishing work one night. But this time, it was just her—no Misa, Hiroko, Jun, or Sunny. Just Kelly. We agreed to go for a drink.

"I only know girl bars," she said, feigning apology, though I took it as a message, loud and clear. She *had* been flirting with me, and I had a decision to make. Do I put an end to the harmless flirting, or do I go through the door she was clearly holding open for me?

I'd always had boyfriends up to that point and had, in fact, just broken up with one, a casualty of my new hours and job focus. Outside of idle fantasy, I had never really considered the possibility of a girlfriend. Then again, I had never ruled it out, either. In fact, I prided myself on trying new things. As my mother was fond of saying when I was growing up, *Wouldn't it be boring if we were all the same?* And since quitting my office job, my entire life was feeling full of possibility and exciting new experiences. Leaving that old uninspiring job and embarking on this new career had been scary and at times humiliating, but it had been nothing if not exhilarating and freeing. My old parameters had been blown apart, along with my barometer of social acceptability. Experience and adventure are good for the soul, I thought. I could—and should—try anything.

"That's okay," I answered nonchalantly, as if lesbian bars were old hat. *As if.* It was just a drink, after all. I wondered how long I would be able to keep my cool.

Once we were at a small table at Henrietta Hudson having drinks, though, everything seemed more difficult and magnified. We no longer had the comfort of a group: no Misa to send secret messages, no Hiroko to fill uncomfortable silences. Conversation suddenly felt like a pretense, a necessary prelude to the business at hand. Or maybe I was just nervous?

"What actors do you like?" she asked.

"Jodie Foster," I offered, the first name that came to mind. Stupid! I do like Jodie Foster, but why couldn't I think of someone, anyone, who isn't gay? I racked my brain. Ellen DeGeneres . . . Melissa Etheridge . . . I didn't even like Melissa Etheridge! She's not even an actor! It was useless. I stopped talking, and when I did, I received confirmation that we were not there for a friendly chat about movie stars; Kelly leaned in to kiss me, and I reciprocated. Easy as pie.

After the kiss, we had a few more drinks, and then she asked if I wanted to "see her apartment." Of course I did. Once there, she offered me a massage (cliché of clichés), which I gladly accepted—I had been on my feet all night, after all. Before long and with the alcohol diluting any anxiety regarding the repercussions of doing *that* with a coworker, our clothes were off.

"OHIO GOZAIMASU!"

These words echoed through the restaurant at that time of day, the hour or so before service started when the waiters started to arrive. *Good morning* was the preferred greeting at Nobu, regardless of arrival time, and I heard the words often while in the thick of preparing the nitty-gritty components of the pastry station: picking mint sprigs, filling and refreshing squeeze bottles, shaving plums, slicing *maki*.

"Ohio!"

My response was instinctive. It was one of only a handful of Japanese words and phrases I had learned, but it was one of my favorites. *Ohio!* was a sufficient abbreviation for greeting a waiter since we were on the same (theoretical) level. I would use the full phrase to greet the sushi chefs, who were not only older than me but also at the top of the kitchen hierarchy.

The exchange was repeated over and over again in a singsong way, and it had a strangely soothing effect on me. Maybe it was all the long vowels. *Oh-hi-oh.* I welcomed its meditative quality. It helped me focus on the simple tasks at hand rather than on the flashes of memory from the night before.

I knew that Kelly was scheduled to work that day, but I didn't see her until after service started, when she walked right by my station to drop off a stack of dirty dishes, looking like she always did. Her shortish black hair was neatly combed away from her face, her thin frame, maybe an inch or two taller than mine, was erect with superb posture. Her features were small—dark, narrow eyes, thin lips, petite nose—but framed by heavy, strong cheekbones. She was wearing the regulation waiter's uniform of khaki pants and navy blue shirt, but all I could see was bare skin, hers and mine, against each other, smooth and soft. In a flash, I remembered the kissing . . . and the touching . . . and the *everything.*

I pretended to focus on the dessert orders that had started to trickle in and prayed that my cheeks had not turned visibly red. (I blush way too easily and it is a curse.) She didn't look me in the eye when she passed me on her way back into the dining room, but I swear I noticed a hairline crack of a smile in her serious but kind face. She was working. I was working. We were too busy to acknowledge last night, but I could not stop thinking about it.

"*Bull-ondie!*" came the welcome distraction from the other end of the kitchen. It was Hisa, one of the sushi chefs, sticking his head into the kitchen from the sushi bar, looking urgently in my direction, his eyebrows raised to the tops of his shaved head.

The sushi chefs were the proverbial kings of the Nobu mountain (unless, of course, Nobu Matsuhisa himself was in town on one of his monthly visits from California, in which case he was emperor). Though Nobu was known for its cooked food as much as its sushi, the sushi chefs were still the stars, performing in the dining room every night, and they knew it. They demanded full attention and usually got it. And if any of the sushi chefs had bothered to learn my name, it would have been news to me. To them, I was just the blond girl.

"Bento box, *cho dai*!" Hisa insisted loudly, pointing to the shelf above my head. I grabbed the oval box and a lid and sent them down to him. He grabbed it and disappeared.

Just as I'd begun to feel like more a part of the fabric that made up the restaurant and less like one of its loose threads threatening to unravel at any moment, I succeeded in positioning myself back on the edge of the unknown. For me, the night with Kelly was casual fun, a sort of litmus test to find out if maybe I had been neglecting a huge pool of potential mates. And while I had enjoyed my night with her, there had been no "*aha!*" moment, no moment of glorious discovery about finally finding what I had been missing all those years. It had been just another hookup. But what had it meant for Kelly? Would she want me to be her girlfriend?

Would she feel scorned when she found out my less than serious intentions?

"Dali-*san*!"

It was Kazu frantically grabbing a ticket off my dupe slide. Or was his name Yoshi? I had trouble remembering all the waiters' names, despite working with them every night; there were so many of them. It was humiliating and embarrassing.

"Dali-*san*!" he said again, smiling. Both my Japanese- and Spanish-speaking coworkers shortened my name to Dali. I guess it was just easier to pronounce.

"I need *Happy Birthday* on this dessert." He circled *position 4* on the ticket, a ginger crème brûlée, and scribbled *HB* at the bottom, as a reminder.

"No problem, Kazu." It was Kazu. Of course! I saw his name printed at the bottom of the ticket.

"Thank you, Dali-*san*." He bowed his head quickly and turned away. I loved that the waiters sometimes addressed me with the endearing and familiar suffix of "*san*," proof that I had been welcomed into the "family," as a group of restaurant employees is called. Some friends whom I was closer to, like Kelly, even used "Dalia-*chan*," an even more familiar term of endearment. I grabbed a plate and the cornet of chocolate. Following the arc of the round plate, I spelled out the birthday wish in smooth, cursive letters, looping the final *y* with a decorative flourish. I marveled at how well I was doing with my chocolate writing. I used to panic at the sight of birthday orders, rushing downstairs for Mika to do it for me. No more.

When I yelled for a pickup, Kazu came quickly, taking the dessert off my hands with a wink. A wink? I looked past him at two other waiters, who were talking quietly in Japanese by the green tea warmer. One of them glanced over at me, then went back to her conversation. Kelly passed by, and they smiled at her, too, though she kept on walking. I tried to listen in on their conversation, straining to hear my name or even *haku-jin,* which means "white person," which could mean me, even if there was an entire dining room full of *haku-jin*s. With all my concerns about last night, it hadn't occurred to me that *other* people might know about it. But of course they would know, I realized with horror. Everybody would know that the new girl (because three months later I was still the new girl) had hooked up with a waiter. We were a *family,* and I had committed an act of lesbian incest.

Thankfully, the nightly stream of orders started rushing in, offering my mind something other than last night (and all of its potential repercussions) to think about. I tried to focus solely on plating the desserts, hoping to replace the flashes of last night in my mind with visions of the plates in front of me. The desserts had become so ingrained in my mind that plating them was almost second nature; I could actually work *and* obsess over last night at the same time. In between endless scoops of green tea and red bean ice cream, I remembered the lights turning off in Kelly's tiny bedroom. As I sent chocolate cakes down the hot line to warm, I recalled waking up in the same small bedroom. I ran downstairs to get more *maki,* and every naked detail came to life. While I was screaming for pickups, torching ginger crème brûlées, and assembling fruit plates, I considered the numerous complications that might result from the night before.

Suddenly, I realized that something was terribly wrong, without full awareness of what that something was. A split second later I felt it, first the searing heat and then the involuntary snapping of my palm off of the freshly burned crème brûlée. Somewhere between the scooping, the fruit plates, and the replaying of the night before, I'd inadvertently let my palm rest on the still-gooey burnt sugar.

I'd been lucky up to that point, and any injuries I suffered at work had been minor. I routinely cut my finger while slicing plums paper thin on the mandoline, an oblong rectangle of plastic fitted with a sharp blade at its middle and sadistically embossed with a warning: *Watch your fingers!* I called it the tool of death. The burns I had gotten so far were superficial, the result of accidentally bumping my hand against a still-hot sheet pan of génoise. That night I crossed into another realm of cuts and burns: I had put my left hand on freshly burnt sugar, which had to have been at least 350 degrees. It was not going to be superficial. I was not going to be able to brush this injury off as I had done the others.

Instinctively, I rubbed my palm on my pant leg, trying to wipe off the browned sugar, but the relative cool of my body and the air had hardened it. Instead, I shoved my palm into my mouth in order to suck off the crusted sugar. Stunned by what I'd done and frozen by the stinging feeling that I knew would soon be searing pain, I felt like Herman, a line cook, who had simply stared blankly after realizing that he'd spilled smoking hot sesame oil onto the back of his hand. The cooks were used to accruing battle scars on a nightly basis, and they were covered, elbow to fingertip, in red marks of varying intensity. Herman's blank stare wasn't indifference, though. It was the anticipation of what he knew would be coming, knowing that it would be worse than any burns he'd gotten before.

And then I felt it: The pain was acute and searing and not at all limited to the large red amoeba that was forming on the outer third of my left palm. Ice. I needed ice. I grabbed a small tub of ice water and lowered my hand into it. This was a fine system, until I noticed the culprit crème brûlée sitting on my counter. I still had tickets to fill.

I removed my hand to have a look. It was just beginning to blister, but that was it—no blood, no missing flesh. No one noticed what had happened, and I knew from watching the cooks burn themselves daily that no one would care about my stupid burn. I would have to tough it out, but it was only a matter of seconds before the numbing effect of the ice water wore off and my hand was again searing with pain. With my left hand back in the tub, I filled a clean side towel with ice and awkwardly wrapped it around the burned area, trying to hold it closed with the same hand. At least I'm right-handed.

I clumsily finished up the rest of the desserts, relieved that the end of the night was near. Jemal, on his way out for the night, stopped and watched me work, my lame clublike hand dripping.

"You should be more careful," he said before walking out the door. There is little sympathy for injuries in the kitchen. They are simply occupational hazards, commonplace and forgettable—things to accept and get past.

When my night was finally over, I left the restaurant quickly, not wanting to have to explain my stupid burn or, worse, talk to anyone, including Kelly, about what happened the night before. Though I could not afford it, I splurged on a cab, taking my bucket of ice water with me.

✦

SIX

Icing on the Cake

Chk! Chk! Chk! Chk! Chk!

I had barely torn the ticket out of the printer when Nami rounded the corner into the pastry station and grabbed it from my hand. She forcefully scribbled the word *Japanese* in bold letters at the bottom of the ticket, next to the preprinted VIP notation from the computer. She underlined it multiple times for effect and barely glanced at me before dropping the ticket on my counter and turning to leave the kitchen. Why did she still bother with her act?

Early on, before I really got the hang of things at Nobu, some people tried to take advantage of me or, worse, even seemed to take pleasure in humiliating me. Haruki, the floor manager, took great pride in pointing out even my tiniest missteps (forgetting a garnish or sending a dessert to the wrong table) in front of the waitstaff. Once he announced, in front of everyone, that a customer had found a blond hair in her food and all but accused me of being unkempt. Jemal assured me that not only was my hygiene more than satisfactory but that Haruki was just an asshole who took pleasure in wielding his tiny amount of power as floor manager to make people feel bad. He had no real influence over my fate as a pastry cook; that honor was Jemal's. If Haruki had been truly concerned, he would have pulled me aside privately to constructively correct.

And then there was Bruce, one of the lead line cooks, who reveled in his inappropriate comments. *Mmmmm . . . so creamy,* he would say lasciviously as I stirred my crème anglaise. He never spoke to me seriously, or even civilly. All I ever got from him were comments and usually when no one else was around: *Ooh, you look good when you come out of the freezer,* he'd say, nodding at my nipples.

And then there was Nami.

Nami was the one waiter who simply refused to accept me. She made no effort to be friendly, took no steps to help me navigate the world in which I was a stranger. Even though the pastry station was under my charge once dinner service began, and I was the one who would be dealing with her special dessert requests, she more often called for Mika, who, once I got a handle on things, spent most of her time tending to more important tasks in the blessed calm of the basement. When she appeared, Nami addressed only Mika and only in Japanese, even when I was standing right there and even long after I'd grown more than capable of handling anything that came my way. I was sure she was complaining about me, worried that a *haku-jin* newbie like me wouldn't have the inner know-how to meet the standards of her "special" Japanese customers. And her VIP special customers were *always* Japanese. To make matters worse, Nami actually complained that I unfairly ate family meal (the communal staff meal that the kitchen made at the end of a shift) twice—once when I came in at two and again at the end of service, around midnight. I rarely ate more than a bowl of rice and some salad—both of which were always in surplus—but that didn't matter to Nami. I was an easy target. She just had to pick on me: the new white girl, the lowest member on the kitchen totem pole.

As I got better at my job and adjusted to life in the kitchen, I figured out that Haruki was probably just cranky from dealing with customers and waiters all night, that Bruce, annoying and inappropriate as he was, was harmless, and that Nami was not to be taken seriously. *That's just Nami,* Mika had said politely when I finally worried aloud about Nami's nasty attitude. It was a condemnation swathed in Mika's inexhaustible civility, but it was enough to bolster my confidence. Enough was enough. After a while, I didn't let Haruki, Bruce, or Nami get to me anymore. I had gotten better at my job, good, even, and I could handle anything.

Nami no longer had my newbie Caucasian butt to push around. I knew that *true* VIPs would be brought to my attention by a manager. I also knew that a customer was not a VIP simply because he or she was Japanese, as Nami's notations implied. She'd try anything to brownnose a customer into giving her a bigger tip. I filled the order as I would have any other. I started by placing a small aluminum tin of molten chocolate cake onto a sizzle platter.

"Bento box!" I screamed, standing at the end of the hot line. It was shorthand for *Please, garde-manger cook, take this sizzle platter of chocolate cake off my hands and pass it down the line until it reaches the oven where the middleman can slide it in.*

Back at my station I finished the other desserts on Nami's ticket. I laid five slices of almond *maki* across a rectangular black slab. Jemal, tired of the chocolate *maki*, had switched it to almond cake with sesame mousse and blueberries inside. On to the Japanese dessert.

I had grown to love the strange elements that Mika incorporated into this ever-evolving dessert: sticky pockets made from rice flour, beans cooked in syrup, candied chestnut fillings. And while she was happy and patient to teach me how to make some of them, like a particular kind of *mochi*—a sticky, gummy dough that was used to wrap all kinds of things—that I loved, she was secretive about others, like her recipe for *ogura,* a sweet red bean paste. Still, she seemed sincerely pleased that I had taken a true liking to Japanese sweets. I loved the textures most of all and the incredible attention to detail. Sometimes Mika would bring in some *wagashi,* the traditional Japanese confections that come wrapped up like perfectly designed gifts and are truly an art. We would take a break, and over some hot green tea, she would explain each exquisite dessert.

I plated that week's traditional Japanese dessert with confidence: a starchy square of mango *kudzu,* a small round of Mika's homemade *ogura,* and a ball of green tea *mochi*–wrapped ice cream cut into quarters with a halved raspberry in its center, all arranged simply and eloquently on a Japanese stoneware plate. The aesthetic was all about clean lines and minimal clutter on the plate. I had it down. I grabbed a small oval bento box from the top shelf of the station and removed its lid. The molten chocolate cake had to be ready by that time.

"Bento, please!"

In a reverse relay, the hot sizzle platter was handed off back down to me. Seiko, my more experienced daytime counterpart who took care of most of the advanced production, had told me earlier that she'd made an especially good batch that morning. By then, I knew what that meant: the molten chocolate cake was bulging up out of its four-ounce tin with the slightest of wiggles still in its center. Perfect. Finally, my internal timer was calibrated and right on target, going off when six or seven minutes had passed. I quickly but carefully and gently inverted the tin into the bento box, letting the fragile cake fall from its container fully intact. If the cake was handled too roughly, it would break open, its chocolate center would prematurely run into a thick pool, and the customer would be robbed of the joy of discovering the cake's hidden surprise center: a melted pool of pure Vahlrona chocolate. It would not be servable, and I would have to start all over again, completely throwing off my cadence for the night.

I quickly scooped a quenelle of green tea ice cream and massaged the metal bulge of the scooper in my warm palm to ensure that the quenelle would fall easily from its scoop in a perfectly smooth oval. A squirt of shiso sauce (shiso is often called Japanese mint, but I think it tastes much more like grassy basil) over the cake and a decorative chocolate oval finished the dessert. I replaced the lid on the bento box, pulled Nami's ticket from the dupe slide, set it on top of the bento box, and started yelling.

"Dessert pickup!"

Nami responded quickly to my call. She *was* efficient, even if she was condescending and unfriendly. She balanced the plate and ceramic slab on one hand and grabbed the bento box with the other, leaving the ticket on my counter.

"*Arigato goazaimas!*" I said cheerfully as she left the kitchen. She hated it when I spoke Japanese, even if it was just to say thank you.

I followed her path to the edge of the dining room. It was late enough that I had completely finished setting up the dessert station but still early enough that not many dessert orders were coming in yet. It was the calm before the storm, and until the small printer started spitting out its crushing mountain of orders, I had a few moments of precious downtime during which I could enjoy the view into the dining room.

As usual, we had a full night of reservations (in almost a year that I spent at Nobu, I can't remember a night on which we did fewer than 275 covers, or people, which meant the restaurant was packed for the entire night) and both the front and back rooms were full. According to our roster of reservations, we would be serving a multitude of VIPs of varying importance that night: rock stars, industry professionals, movie stars, investors, movie stars/investors. Their reservations were noted on the VIP list before service so that everyone would know that they were to be paid special attention. At the very least, they would receive an extra dessert, on the house. I learned that dessert was the "freebie" of choice most of the time. Desserts were low-cost items, as their ingredients were invariably inexpensive (how much do flour, sugar, even chocolate, cost compared to meat, fish, and specialty produce?), and were often thought of as special treats, bonuses that customers might otherwise forgo.

From my post at the edge of the kitchen, I could see into the *other* half of the restaurant, the front of the house, which was a sensory contrast to the kitchen in every way. The lights were soft and flattering, large windows looked out onto the Tribeca streets, modern "trees" made from stained planks of wood adorned various corners, the tablecloth-free wooden tabletops—everything about the room, save the excitement of the customers and the insistence of the waiters, felt calm and relaxed.

I could see Robert De Niro (famous movie star/investor #1) already seated at his favored table in the back corner of the back room, chatting over sushi with Harvey Keitel (famous movie star #2). They were both regulars. Brad Pitt and Gwyneth Paltrow would be arriving later on. The restaurant was so popular with the rich and famous, so regularly inundated with notable names, that I grew accustomed to the constant influx of celebrity. I never actually met any of the stars, unlike the star sushi chefs. They actually worked *in* the dining room, and could have conversations with them if it seemed appropriate. Morimoto once left his post, ran downstairs, and changed into his street clothes just so he could say hello to Ralph Lauren while wearing his head-to-toe Ralph Lauren ensemble. Then he changed back and returned to work. I once bumped into Bill Murray, when we both happened to exit the restrooms at the same time. He complimented me on a job well done, and went back to his table. After so many months of serving celebrities, I was more impressed with his height than anything else. Outside of that, my relationship with celebrity—with all customers, really—was that of servant-master: they demanded, I served. We communicated via computer-generated tickets or anxious waiter. Mel Gibson wanted to send Rene Russo an "obscene" dessert as a joke? I did my best and cut a long rod of *maki*, stood it on a plate like a tower, set two balls of *mochi* ice cream at its base, and spooned some crème anglaise around it. I liked to think that no matter how famous or important the VIPs were, they still needed me if they wanted dessert. I could do something they couldn't.

Chk! Chk! Chk! Chk! Chk!

The sound pulled me out of the dining room and back to my post with Pavlovian force as the printer began its nightly crescendo and jettisoned its white paper tongue: six tables at once. Time to focus. I tallied the dessert totals: three almond *maki*, five bento boxes, two fruit plates (damn the time-consuming fruit plates! Why couldn't people just throw caution to the wind, live a little, and order a *real* dessert?), one ginger crème brûlée, and one *kotaishi maki*. *Kotaishi maki* was Jemal's latest addition to the menu. Unlike the almond *maki*, the *kotaishi maki* was actually two tall cylinders of striped green tea and almond cake, cut on the bias and filled with mango-chocolate mousse, and served with coconut-ginger broth. It was the first dessert to appear on the menu that I actually didn't like, mostly because of the thin broth that pooled around the towers. After tasting it for the first time, I'd swallowed quietly and just nodded, afraid to tell the truth while being absolutely incapable of lying (another curse I live with). Not that it mattered, since Jemal's confidence was unwavering and seemingly indestructible. I wondered if I'd ever be so self-assured.

I made all twelve desserts at once. I learned long ago that it is just as easy, and faster, to make five bento boxes at once (or *maki* or brûlées) as it is to make one. I lined my narrow counter with their respective plates and loaded two sizzle platters with molten chocolate cakes. The bento box was quickly becoming Nobu's signature dessert.

"Bento boxes for the oven!" I bellowed from the end of the line, no longer shy about yelling in the kitchen.

For the next two hours or so, until the printer finally slowed down, I was a whirlwind of measured movement: assessing tickets as they came in, timing the molten cakes, decoratively cutting fruit. In between, I rapidly replenished sauce bottles, sliced *maki* for backup, and moved stacks of warm just-washed plates into the cooler so they would be chilled in time for plating. Ice cream on a warm plate turns into a soupy mess, and if I forgot to refill my stack in the refrigerator, I ended up wasting valuable time chilling plates with ice and towel-drying them. I did not have that kind of time. I finally understood what Linda had meant: Work in the kitchen was all about timing, using every moment as efficiently as possible, not wasting a single second.

I responded to urgent calls of "Dali-*san!*" from frantic waiters who had forgotten to punch in their dessert orders and who needed them five minutes earlier. Those tickets got prioritized to the front of the line, as did those tickets with a single quickly plated dessert unfortunately caught between a bevy of large tables. A customer should not have to wait fifteen minutes for a single crème brûlée just because he or she ordered right after two time-consuming large tables. The waiters and I worked in tandem to ensure that the customers enjoyed their final course, that their last moments in the restaurant were as exceptional as those that led up to them. The better the waiters did their job (ordering concisely and efficiently, noting special requests legibly and as early as possible), the better I was at satisfying their requests and vice versa.

The crush, as usual, lasted a full two hours, and when the tide of orders finally began to recede, I made a quick assessment of the station. I refilled squeeze bottles, shaved more plum into the remaining pool of ginger syrup, removed any broken, unusable pieces from the container of tuiles. Now that it was later in the evening, I would have more time between orders, so I didn't bother cutting any more fruit. Instead, I started consolidating and cleaning out nearly empty vessels, deciding what could be saved for tomorrow's lunch service and what leftovers should be given to the family at end of the night. Waiters are always more than happy to eat dessert scraps.

Jemal, who had been working downstairs, came bounding into the kitchen. He preferred working at night, when he could enjoy the quiet solitude of the empty basement since the rest of us were upstairs. That month, his hair was electric blue, like a Smurf.

"Here." He handed me a small, diamond-shaped piece of dark chocolate.

"*Yuzu*," he said. "I just made them."

The chocolate was dark and shiny, with two thin stripes of white chocolate decorating its top. He often made hand-molded chocolates as a treat for VIP customers. It was a delight to watch him temper simple slabs of chocolate or boxes of *pistoles* (chocolate that came in small drops) and turn them into beautifully shiny miniature works of edible art. Tempering the chocolate (melting it down and then re-emulsifying the fats and sugars) made it easier to work with and gave it a more appetizing shiny surface. He would gently heat the chocolate to around 118 degrees, then cool it down by adding unmelted chocolate, stirring until it reached around 92 degrees, depending on how high the cocoa content was. *It's like magic!* I told him the first time I had watched. *No, Dalia,* he said, sternly holding my stare. *Pastry is magic.*

Jemal always judged the temperature of melted chocolate by lifting his rubber spatula directly from the chocolate to his lower lip, *feeling* the temperature. He scoffed at any notion that this was unsanitary, and started testing me on my temperature-judging abilities. I always thought it was cool enough when it was actually still at least 10 degrees too warm. *Keep practicing, Dalia,* he told me, *Repetition . . . repetition.*

He loved working with chocolate, though he complained that neither the customers nor the waiters amply appreciated his work. At first I thought that he was just being a prima donna, that no amount of appreciation would ever be enough. When someone accidentally (or, more likely, carelessly) unplugged his small refrigerator, set at the perfect temperature to keep the chocolates shiny (temperatures too hot or too cold cause chocolate to "bloom," turn cloudy or spotted on its surface), Jemal was rightfully angered and demoralized by the waste of all his time, but the rest of the kitchen barely shrugged, let alone apologized. Sadly, I learned that it *was* true what they'd told me long ago: Cooks just don't care about pastry.

Jemal believed that everyone, especially pastry people, should eat at least one piece of chocolate every day. But, after being given a license early on to eat whatever I wanted from the pastry station, I'd quickly made myself ill from green tea *mochi,* dessert *maki,* and mini fig tarts. He knew that chocolate was the last thing I wanted to eat, even if it was filled with *yuzu,* one of my favorite new Japanese flavors, which tastes a lot like a more complex, super Meyer lemon crossed with mandarin orange with a tiny hint of salt.

I took the chocolate, but as he turned to fill an earthenware mug with green tea (we all drank a lot of green tea at Nobu) I nonchalantly dropped the chocolate into the trash, hoping it would take cover beneath a paper towel. I kept my mouth shut, ignoring Jemal.

He headed back downstairs, paused to look into the trash, then looked at me, determined.

"I'll bring you another one, since you dropped that," he said definitively.

Itaru, a sushi chef, caught my eye from the end of the line. Holding a small bento box of his own, he offered it to me with a nod of his head and sent it down the line to me. It was a game we sometimes played at the end of night, a mutual reward for busy service.

Itaru was the sixth sushi chief, an appendage to the set of five who already performed nightly at the sushi bar, a stage that was only large enough for five. He was instead placed at a tiny scrap of counter space at the end of the kitchen line directly outside the doorway between the hot line and the sushi bar. He was an "extra" chef, handing out various pieces of sushi, sashimi, and other garnishes to the other sushi chefs. He was a quiet, efficient chef and, unlike most of the other sushi chefs, incredibly friendly. He also had an insatiable sweet tooth that he satisfied by way of trade with me. I returned his nod and made my way down the line to receive the bento box.

I removed the lid to the small lacquer box to find a small piece of dark, coral-colored salmon sushi; a piece of *hamachi,* yellowtail in the palest of lavender hues; and three thick, square slabs of *tomago,* the slightly sweet chilled omelet that I especially liked to snack on. My interest in sushi had been slow in coming; I'd never even eaten it before working at Nobu. Mika eased me into it, laughing gently at my request to not try anything too fishy. It sounded ridiculous to her; it was fish, after all! But like much of my experience at Nobu, once I got it, I *got* it. My gift from Itaru was the perfect late-night nosh to enjoy while waiting for the final dessert orders to come in, after which I could finally close down my station and head home or go out for a drink. Happy hour for me, for anyone in the restaurant business, started at midnight. Until then, though, I was at the mercy of those final customers who wanted to linger over the last of their sake, completely unaware that while they put off their decision to have dessert, I could be missing the next train home or the shared taxi to the bar across town.

After finishing my sushi snack, I cleaned out the box; filled it with slices of chocolate *maki, mochi* ice cream, some green tea tuiles, and the second *yuzu* chocolate that Jemal had forced on me; and returned it to Itaru. He smiled broadly when he opened the box back at his end of the kitchen.

Ten months earlier I was burning cakes and pots, dropping stacks of plates, doing virtually everything wrong. I used to live in constant fear that I would be fired at any moment. I struggled with adapting to my new lifestyle: the late hours, the social hierarchy, the physicality, the injuries. It had been a slow progression—at times a torturous one—but one I had managed to figure out and even master.

In two weeks, though, my culinary school program would come to an end, and I would begin my search for a part-time culinary externship, the last step in my formal culinary education, after which I would finally leave Nobu for a cooking job. I would miss Itaro and our exchange game, green tea, *yuzu, wagashi* breaks, bento boxes, unfamiliar tastes, and the now familiar sound of Japanese. Mika and Jemal had always known the time would come, that my time in pastry was temporary. It seemed sad that just as I had really gotten the hang of things, it was time to move on. I would have to start all over again.

SEVEN

✦

Salad Days

Most of the people in my culinary program began their search for an externship by looking over the long list of restaurants and corporate dining rooms that participated with the school's externship program. Some students jumped eagerly at the tiny number that actually offered a small pittance of payment; others went for those that offered the shortest commute. After working for almost a year at a three-star restaurant, I wanted quality. I also needed to keep my full-time job at Nobu at least until I completed my externship so I could continue paying my rent, so I needed something that would fit into my work schedule.

At first, I was set on advancing my cooking career while getting closer to my Danish background, but a trail at Aquavit, New York's only three-star Scandinavian restaurant, left me feeling uninspired. Though the food was innovative (smoked avocado, espresso mustard, goat cheese sorbet), delicious, and meticulously executed, the kitchen vibe just didn't feel right. Maybe I'd grown too accustomed to Mika's gentle guidance and Jemal's genuine interest in teaching. When Steven, one of the senior managers at Nobu, suggested I do my externship at Layla, a restaurant owned by the same restaurant group as Nobu and just a block away, it made sense. I'd get to extern two days a week at a great restaurant (the recently opened Layla had just received a glowing two-star review from the *New York Times*), and Nobu would be flexible with my schedule. Steven walked me over himself.

"Here she is, Joey," Steven said, handing me off to Layla's chef.

Layla was a large corner restaurant with enormous windows, hanging lantern–style lights, and lots of colorful tiles. As we sat in one of the booths, Joey gave me a brief overview of his style. He'd trained both in New York and Paris, so his food was rooted in traditional cooking methods, but he favored the flavors of the Mediterranean, including Italian, which was his heritage. Layla's food spanned both Mediterranean Europe and the Middle East, so he incorporated many of the flavors and ingredients of the region—zaatar, couscous, sumac, phyllo—in a way that seemed completely natural.

As I sat listening to Joey, I tried to get a feeling for the place (after all, a "feeling" had turned me off to Aquavit and another "feeling" had motivated me to enroll in cooking school). The dining room was full of natural light that bled into the completely open kitchen which extended out from the long, curved bar. I could hear music, Oasis's "Champagne Supernova," playing in the kitchen. The cooks were smiling, and they seemed calm. One of them was a woman.

"We got nice people working here," Joey said, "but we work hard and we make good food."

"Okay," I said. My decision was made.

For the next month, I spent my two days off as well as a few of my mornings at Layla, arriving at nine a.m. and staying well into the evening for service. Most of the time I served as an extra pair of hands and did whatever little task anyone needed (or, more often, hated doing themselves): brunoising sticky, dried apricots for the *bastiya*, juicing zucchini for the Israeli couscous, plucking pomegranate seeds. I became the phyllo flower "queen." Jessica, the sauté cook, hated making the ruffled phyllo flower garnish for her *bastiya*, but I, apparently, was good at it. The flowers became part of my routine there, and she was happy not to have to deal with them. *When you're here,* she said, complimenting me, *my whole stress level just drops.*

My pastry experience often landed me at the pastry station during service. Though it was the one place I felt confident (plating desserts was second nature by that point), it also made me slightly uncomfortable. I just didn't think the desserts at Layla were as good as those at Nobu. All the plates looked the same: something plopped in the middle of the plate and surrounded by sauce. The chocolate cake was thick and dense, not airy and oozing like the bento box cake, and in my opinion they used an inferior brand of chocolate. I felt guilty for being such a snob after hardly a year in the business, so I kept quiet and did whatever they asked.

I'd been externing for about a month when, rather suspiciously, the cooks started dropping hints. *You'd fit in great here,* Juan, the bread station cook, told me in the privacy of the walk-in refrigerator. He manned the brick oven that bulged into the dining room. *Joey's a great chef,* and *he's a nice guy. You'll really be able to learn at a place like this,* Jessica quietly advised. Even Chris, the rough and burly daytime sous-chef, put in his two cents: *We got a real good crew here,* he announced. By the time Joey sat me down and officially offered me the position of garde-manger, all of their "subtle" encouragement had worked its magic. I took the job.

It was the last time for a long while that Joey talked to me for more than two minutes at a time. It hadn't taken me long to figure out that all the women at Layla had crushes on Joey. I was far too intimidated by him to consider him in any role other than that of chef. I made no attempt to be his friend, I just wanted to do a good job. In any case, he barely spoke to me, and when he did, I was usually flummoxed. He once asked me if I'd been "one of the smart kids" in high school. Not knowing the correct answer, I just shrugged. *It's the smart ones you gotta worry about, Dolly,* he said cryptically and without context, and walked away, leaving me panicked. Didn't he think I was smart enough to make it? Or, was I *too* smart to succeed in the virtually nonintellectual arena of the kitchen? He was a mystery to me. Far more worrisome, though, were his oblique comments related to my position in his kitchen.

"So, Dolly . . ." said Joey, edging up to me while I organized the various bins of greens I needed for service. He insisted on being called Joey, not Chef, and in the two months I'd been working at Layla I never heard him called anything else. He also insisted on adding a final "ee" to everyone *else's* name, too, which unfortunately made me Dolly, even on the official schedule.

"Yeah, Joey?" I answered apprehensively.

As he stood next to me, I kept my head down and continued picking through my bin of mesclun, searching for the imperfect greens that had become the bane of my garde-manger existence. Garde-manger, an entry-level position and the lowest in the kitchen line, is responsible for the cold appetizers, including salads—things that require the least amount of skill. I spent what seemed like hours picking through piles of leaves searching for any that were starting to brown, wilt, or, worse, slime—any that might have gotten in the way of my nightly quest for salad perfection.

"Dolly," Joey said again, "what do you want to be when you grow up?"

When I grew up? I was twenty-five years old. And wasn't it obvious? I wanted to be a chef. Or something.

"*Um* . . ." I answered feebly, "I don't know."

I was useless.

"I mean," I stammered, trying to recover, "I want to cook." Duh.

"Okay, Dolly," he answered.

That was it?

"Just wondering," he said, lingering at my side. I turned nervously back to my greens and folded a clean, dry side towel over them, lovingly tucking them in the way Joey had showed me. Why was he still standing there?

"So," he finally said. "You have a special tonight."

Back to business.

"Vine-ripened tomato," he said officially, raising his chin slightly, as if he were announcing royalty, "stuffed with a grilled Gulf shrimp and escabeche salad, with curry oil and balsamic reduction."

Uh-oh.

"All you need to do is get the tomatoes ready and grill the shrimp," he said. "Jessie will show you how. The rest of the *mise-en-place* is downstairs in the walk-in."

"Okay," I answered, but he was already walking away.

Jessie worked the sauté station, and, thanks to both her calm demeanor and talent, she'd been my best source of help since I had started. She patiently answered my endless insecure questions and never made me feel stupid for asking in the first place. After five minutes and a quick chat with her, I was standing on the hot line, fifteen scored vine-ripened tomatoes and a bowl of ice water at my side, waiting for my pot of water to boil and still wondering what to make of that strange conversation. My year at Nobu had given me a bit of confidence, enough to keep at bay the fear of being fired at any moment. It had taught me the importance of organization, preparedness, and efficiency, and I'd put those skills to use at my new job at Layla. As far as I could tell, I hadn't yet made any major mistakes.

I came in early every day to make sure I'd have enough time to be prepared by the time service started at five thirty p.m. I was responsible for all of the cold appetizers on the menu, which included all of the *mezze* and salads, thirteen items in all, half of which required the use of the Robot Coupe, a heavy-duty commercial-strength food processor that we lovingly referred to as R2-D2. My predecessor was unimpressed with the responsibilities of garde-manger. *I didn't spend two years in culinary school just to make dips,* he'd said scornfully under his breath when I was still an extern, but to me it was just the first step on the way up. It was my chance to make an impression as a real cook making real food for paying customers in a real restaurant for a real chef.

For weeks I hounded my more experienced coworkers, toting around a Robot Coupe filled with hummus (or baba ghanoush or herbed feta). *Does this taste right? More tahini? More salt? More lemon juice?* Unlike the dessert production at Nobu, there were no recipes, only lists of ingredients and basic methods. Everything was done by taste. After taste. After taste. Slowly, slowly, I gained confidence in my taste buds and my instincts. Surely Joey had noticed that it no longer took me an hour to make hummus because of all the second-guessing, hadn't he? And that I was always, always, set up and ready for service? That I kept my station clean and organized?

Some things *had* become second nature to me, like blanching vegetables and salting my water. I threw in a handful of kosher salt (rule: always salt the water, salty like the sea). Once the water reached a full boil, I gently lowered in the tomatoes.

What had Joey meant, *What do you want to be when you grow up?* Did he think that cooking was just a temporary thing for me, a hobby? Or did he simply think I wasn't cut out for it, as in *What do you want to be when you grow up, Dolly . . . 'cause you sure do suck at this?* Was he questioning my commitment? Wondering if I was an employee worth investing in? Why hadn't I told him that I *love* cooking? *Actually, Joey,* I should have said, *I've wanted to be a chef for as long as I can remember. I read cookbooks when I was twelve! I made crêpes from scratch for my friends in high school . . . for fun! Oh, and by the way, I am* already *grown up and this* is *what I want to do. I gave up a safe, stable office job for this!* No, I hadn't said any of that. As usual, I hadn't been able to think that quickly.

I might not have been so worried if I had ever gotten some sort of concrete positive reinforcement, a single moment of serious conversation when Joey actually commented on my job performance. But no, that's not how it worked. Joey's biggest contribution to my self-confidence thus far had been to nonchalantly dip a pinky into one of my *mezze* and mutter "quality control" before popping the finger into his mouth and walking away. No "yum," no "perfect," not even a "Good job, Dolly." Only what sometimes felt like an interminable daily grind in which I had no choice but to believe that no news was good news.

It only took a minute or two for the tomato skins to start peeling away from the shallow *X*s I had sliced into the bottom of each one. I lifted them out of the water with a spider (a round wire-mesh tool with a long handle) and placed them in the bowl of ice water I had waiting (rule: always use ice water to stop the cooking).

While my tomatoes cooled, I moved on to the shrimp. After tossing them in olive oil, I sprinkled them evenly with salt and twisted the wooden pepper mill over them, giving the grayish crustaceans a generous dusting of freshly ground white pepper (rule: season everything with salt and pepper). One by one, I lined them up on the hot grill.

"Hurry up, Dolly!" urged Mina, who suddenly appeared at the grill station, her station.

Mina had started back when I was an extern. *She's Jewish and Peruvian, and she can cook,* Jessie had told me excitedly. *And she speaks Spanish.* She was younger than me but had already worked in great restaurants for years. Mina bent her knees to lower the heavy stack of half sheet trays on the counter, each one fully loaded with a single layer of the meats and fishes she would need for her station.

"I gotta grill my chickens!"

Where Jessie was all about delicate touch and calm determination, Mina was just the opposite. She had an edgy energy more like a machine in overdrive and had no qualms about bossing me—or anyone—around if she felt it necessary. She had contempt for anyone "soft," and on the rare occasion a waiter burned him- or herself by grabbing a hot plate from behind the line she had no sympathy. *It's a kitchen,* she would say matter-of-factly, and shrug. *Everything's hot.* I had managed to stay on her good side, and she was friendly most of the time, so I didn't take her bossing personally. She *did* know what she was doing. She grabbed the tongs impatiently from me and deftly began turning three and four shrimp at a time before handing the tongs back to me, lesson accomplished. (I had turned them one at a time—much too time consuming.) Sometimes I had to be taught the most obvious of things.

It only took another thirty seconds or so before all the shrimp turned opaque—just cooked through—and I could get out of her way. Using her three-at-a-time method, I loaded the cooked shrimp onto a half sheet to cool, then cleaned the grill with a few quick swipes of the grill brush before leaving her station. Mina gave an approving nod (rule: you use it, you clean it).

Back at my station, I took the cooled tomatoes out of the ice water and swiftly peeled them, cut out the lids, scooped out the insides with my fingers, arranged them upside down on a towel-lined half sheet tray (lids on the side), and slid them into my low-boy. It was five thirty-five p.m., and from my station, an extension of the bar, I could see silhouettes of the first customers coming through the sunny, glass-fronted entrance of the restaurant. Early birds. I had to stop obsessing over Joey's cryptic messages and focus on service.

I gave my station a once-over. Hummus, baba ghanoush, *tadzhiki,* tabouleh, *taramasalata,* white bean puree, herbed feta, cumin-spiced carrots. Check. Bins of frisée and mesclun, cleaned and picked through. Check. Dolmas, vegetarian and lamb, both heating up. I had backups of everything. I found two empty squeeze bottles and filled one with the neon yellow curry oil, the other with a dark, syrupy balsamic vinegar reduction.

"Olives for four," said a waiter, walking by. Olives already.

As soon as diners were seated, they got a small bowl of marinated olives and white bean dip for their table. We went through so many olives that Joey marinated them with his secret combination of spices downstairs in an enormous tub that was big enough for me to bathe in. I kept a smaller stash of them at my station for service. I spooned some olives into a small bowl and some of the garlicky rosemary bean dip into another one and set them on the bar of my station to be picked up. Until it got busy, the waiters would casually walk by, declaring their olive and bean dip needs, which I in turn would fill. Sometimes they would even thank me. But as the night progressed and the crunch set in, their requests would start to sound more like angry demands. *Olives for two! For six! Olives for four, twice! Olives! Olives! Olives! I need olives!* Their frenetic requests used to intimidate me, but after a while I found their madness almost amusing; they rattled so easily.

"You got a hummus and a baba, Dolly," Joey said, standing at the edge of my station. "And you got a special coming your way." He stuck a yellow copy of the ticket onto my dupe slide before returning to his post in front of the printer, across from the hot line. "Pull out the *mise-en-place,*" he added. "I'll be back in a sec to show you the plate."

I grabbed the appropriate dishes for the hummus and baba and spooned a dollop of each into their respective bowls. The hummus got a small well of extra-virgin olive oil and lemon juice and was topped with finely chopped red onion, toasted pignoli nuts, and chopped chives. The smoky baba, a roasted eggplant dip, got a sprinkle of chopped black olives, tomato *concassé,* and chopped parsley. And then, just to be sure, because it had been that kind of a day, I dipped my finger into the hummus, then into my mouth. Delicious. It wasn't until I set the small plates on the bar for pickup that I noticed the two guys sitting farther down at the bar, drinks in hand.

I saw that, one of them mouthed with a self-satisfied grin. I smiled weakly at them, wiping my finger on a side towel. Most of the time I loved working in an open kitchen—being able to see the diners, look out the windows, and hear the music—but every once in a while we got someone with an obnoxious comment. *If you're afraid of people touching your food,* I wanted to sneer back, *don't eat in a restaurant.*

"Don't worry about them, Dolly," said Joey, who had suddenly appeared at my side. He dipped his knuckle into the baba and, nodding at the dorks at the bar, licked the baba off of it. More "quality control."

"Perfect," he said, as much to the guys at the bar as to me. It took two losers at the bar to drag out a compliment.

"So," he said, looking at me. "Grab a plate."

I pulled a chilled white plate from the lowboy (greens, like ice cream, work best on chilled plates) and set it on the counter next to the rest of the *mise-en-place* I had already gathered nearby.

Joey grabbed a small bunch of the juicy escabeche, paper-thin slices of red and yellow pepper, red onions, and fennel that were marinated in lemon, lime, and orange juices and extra-virgin olive oil, and dropped it into the bowl with the frisée.

"Season it, like always," he said.

I sprinkled salt and ground some white pepper over the bowl while he gave it a quick mix.

"Make a little bed for the tomato to sit on." He spread a dab of the mixture onto the middle of the plate and set a tomato in the center of it. He added four grilled shrimp to the remaining salad and used that to stuff the tomato, letting two of the shrimp peek out of the top.

"You gotta show off the shrimp," he said before finally placing a tomato "lid" on top. "They're beautiful, right, Dolly?

"Then, curry oil and balsamic reduction. Make dots all around the tomato." He handed me the two squeeze bottles. "Just think of Seurat," he said, giving me a nudge with his elbow. "I love Seurat."

I held one squeeze bottle over the plate, letting bright yellow dots of curry oil fall onto the plate, then followed with the dark balsamic reduction, filling the leftover white space. They looked like miniature oil slicks.

"Looks great, Doll," he said, smiling. "You've got a good eye."

I wiped the edges of the freshly plated special and set it on the bar next to the hummus and baba ghanoush that went with it. Maybe my initiation period of uncertainty and insecurity was coming to an end. Maybe the whole day had been some sort of a test.

"Who knows, Dolly," said Joey just before he walked away. "Maybe you'll end up being a food stylist."

I swear I saw him wink.

✦

EIGHT

In the Line of Fire

After a couple of months, I mastered garde-manger. My station was immaculately organized, my *mezze* were perfectly seasoned, and I never ran out of anything. Ever. Mina and Jessie even started raiding my station at the end of the night for a snack, scraping out the leftover hummus and baba with grilled bread, saying my *tadzhiki* was the best. I had been in the weeds during service only once, and even then it was because Joey had given me fresh oysters as a special. They were insanely popular, and with six orders picking up at once (thirty-six oysters to shuck in one shot!), I fell behind, despite my surprising deftness at shucking. Joey seemed to enjoy my frantic shucking and smiled sadistically every time he called out yet another order of oysters. Another "test," no doubt, to see if I could handle the pressure. I did.

In the meantime, Sprout, my predecessor in garde-manger, had moved up to the next station: hot appetizer. Mina dubbed him Sprout because she thought the few hairs left on his prematurely balding head looked like plugs. He'd earned her disdain by mistakenly soaking a huge bucket of hazelnuts instead of garbanzo beans for the falafel. She instantly wrote him off as a hack who wouldn't make it. When Mina decided that she didn't like someone, she showed no mercy: *They don't call me Meany for nothing,* she always said. I was lucky to have stayed on her good side.

When Sprout gave his notice, none of us was sorry to see him go, especially me. In my mind he was the worst kind of cook: bitter about not advancing quickly but still too arrogant to admit he didn't know enough. He once identified something to me as cracked red lentil rather than admit he simply didn't know. I found out later it was dried lobster roe. His departure meant the vacating of the hot appetizer station, a spot I'd had my eye on. I was ready to make the move but unsure of how to proceed. Did I tell Sprout? Encourage Jessie and Meany to put in a good word for me? Go directly to Joey? Or was it up to Joey to decide that I was ready? And what about Juan? Juan worked the bread station, baking pita and a few other appetizer items to order in a brick oven that jutted into the dining room. He'd been working at Layla longer than I. Did he have priority? If I had learned anything by that time, it was that nothing was obvious or logical when it came to kitchen protocol.

Joey decided to give both Juan and me a chance to work hot app, as we called it. For a while we alternated on the station (we were being tested and compared, I was sure) until finally he decided that Juan would work Sunday through Wednesday and I would work Thursday through Saturday, the busier days. I had aced the test.

Once on hot app I was finally working with fire, actually cooking food to order for customers instead of simply spooning *mezze* I'd made earlier into little bowls or arranging shrimp I had cooked long before the immediacy of service had begun. And it was a challenge. Working with fire meant that everything had to be timed perfectly; overcooked food could not be served. I had to work with two other stations—grill and sauté—to make sure that we put up all of a single table's food at the same time. And while the main focus of hot app was appetizers that required cooking, the station was also responsible for preparing two entrées: Cinnamon-Braised Lamb Shank with Israeli Couscous and Seafood Couscous Royale. They were supposed to be two of the easier entrées, meaning they didn't require the more advanced skill needed on the grill or sauté stations, but they didn't feel so easy to me. While cooking Israeli couscous "risotto" style, I might have to simultaneously gently heat the fragile yogurt sauce for the *manti,* a lamb ravioli appetizer, or pass an order of *boereks,* small pockets of phyllo filled with feta cheese and fresh herbs, over to Juan at the bread station. If I burned something and had to do it over, it could mess up the timing for an entire table, or screw up an entire pickup. It was a lot of pressure, but I loved it.

I loved the bouquet the garlic released when it first hit the hot pan. I loved the magic of mussels and clams opening up from the steam of white wine pooled beneath them. I loved sautéing head-on shrimp and steaming lobster tails. I loved the thrill of mounting in whole butter (stirring it into a hot liquid to create a sauce) and melding the flavors together with just the perfect amount of salt and pepper to create the finished dish: Seafood Couscous Royale.

I developed a very close relationship with the deep fryer, into which I fed a seemingly constant stream of the insanely popular (and delicious) curried crab rolls. The smell of hot canola oil seeped into my clothes, my hair, and my skin, and stayed there until I showered the next morning. I was usually too exhausted from drinking late into the night after work to do anything but fall into bed when I got home.

But odors weren't my only souvenir. Burns became an inherent part of my life once I started working on hot app, and I quickly learned to accept the blisters, scars, and pain as simple occupational hazards (unlike my crème brûlée burn at Nobu, which was the result of sheer carelessness and distraction). We all had them; every cook does.

"Nice one, Doll," Joey said one night, nodding approvingly at the forearm I'd just splattered with hot oil. I had dropped an order of falafel into the fryer without first lifting its basket out of the oil (I was trying to save time). The impressive burn was amorphic, the size of a silver dollar, red-rimmed and already bulging with liquid. It was my first bad burn earned on the hot line and worthy of recognition. My only purpose in life was to prepare the food as efficiently as Joey demanded, without compromising a single detail. I'd gotten all my food out on time, I had worked cleanly, and my plates had looked beautiful. The food off my station had gone out well, and my freshly burned forearm was evidence that I'd prioritized the food over my own safety, and Joey had noticed. His approval was everything to me, and his acknowledgment was nothing less than a verbal pat on the back, a congratulation, a brief moment of common ground. I'd worked on the hot line with the other "real" cooks, and I'd done all right. I was one of them.

Outsiders often wonder why we don't use oven mitts. The thick, awkward mittens would turn our hands—our most important tools—into useless padded lobster claws. And though the use of insulated mitts might prevent a burn or two, the teasing they would spur would far outweigh their benefit. You might as well wear a sign that says I'M AFRAID OF FIRE! You, along with those clueless softies who use extra-long tongs in order to stay a safe distance away from the heat, would be dubbed a "pussy." And worse, if you were a woman in a room full of men (or women like Mina, who dish it out as much as they receive it), there would be a resounding *Figures,* and your efforts to prove yourself would be further thwarted, as if it weren't already difficult enough.

Burn cream? Even if you could take the time in the middle of a rush to do a little bit of self-tending, creams do little to ease the pain, especially when the wound has hours of close proximity to a flame to endure, and even then you'd have to worry about the cream getting into the food. Any attempt to prevent scarring would be futile anyway and vain—and vanity has no place in the kitchen. Burns are instead worn proudly like badges of honor, symbols of service in the line of fire. They are reminders that we remained tough with our kitchen team through the heat and sweat, and did it all without complaining. Complaining is for sissies. And waiters. Once I became a more seasoned line cook, waiters lost some of their charm.

Most cooks believe that while they're working hard pursuing dream careers in the kitchen, waiters are simply biding their time working in restaurants to fund their own dream careers elsewhere. Waiters are frustrated actors, artists, dancers, and, in the mind of most cooks, whiners. They complain about everything: They don't make enough money, they're tired, their feet hurt, they feel too sick to work. God forbid one of them gets a paper cut or breaks a nail punching in an order. Every complaint is an insult to cooks who, nine times out of ten, work longer, harder, and for substantially less money. During work hours, cooks have no patience for whining waiters, and more than one kitchen I've worked in has had a NO CRYING IN THE KITCHEN sign posted. Of course, none of this stops all kinds of after-hours contact. Once work is over and the drinks are poured, the playing field is leveled.

After a few months on hot app, my forearms were riddled with burns of varying degree and size. My father wondered if, taking the subway home late at night, smelly, dirty, and with forearms full of scars, people weren't afraid to sit next to me, since I looked like a junkie. But I didn't care about the burns, the sweat, the dirt, or the smell; I was cooking.

✦

NINE

Ladies' Night

Not long after I started working on hot app, Meany became the sous-chef. This led to some temporary tension between her and Jessie, who had been working at Layla longer and had also wanted the position. *It was a tough decision, Dolly,* Joey confided in me, during another one of his enigmatic monologues. *Jessie is creative . . . has a good eye, good ideas. But Meany, Meany is such a hard worker. If I could just put them together I'd have the perfect person.* I took this to mean that I could learn something from both of them, that I should try to be that perfect hybrid. Meany's promotion also meant that the grill station position would be available.

"It won't be easy, Dolly," Joey said. "This is the hard-core stuff. The Wild, Wild West of restaurant cooking." He paused for effect. "It's a busy station. You gotta learn your temps."

I considered this. The entrées on hot app did not require cooking meat to a desired temperature, which was precisely why they
were relegated to the hot app station. The lamb shank was braised
(cooked for almost three hours until the meat fell off the bone),
and the shellfish was, well, shellfish. It just got cooked: Clams and
mussels opened when they were done and shrimp turned opaque.
Meat temperatures were mysterious.

"And it's fucking hot over there, and I mean HOT. You gotta
be able to take the heat."

How much hotter could it get? I was already sweltering over
the fryer and burners in hot app.

"But," he finally said, dangling the position in front of me, "if
you think you can handle it . . ."

He was challenging me; I knew it.

"I can handle it," I said without hesitation. Any insinuation that
I wouldn't be up to the task only made me more determined.

It turned out that the grill *was* a whole other level of cooking.
It *was* fucking hot over the grill, so hot that I sometimes felt like
I was working over a volcano. There was no escape from the fire
and smoke, only the respite of gallons of cold water to drink. Virtually every item on my station could be cooked to a variety of
degrees. I had to keep all the information organized in my head,
and all my proteins on my grill organized too. Toughest of all, as
I had been warned, I had to learn to judge temperature by feel.

"You just gotta get used to it, Dolly," Meany, my grill coach,
told me. By then everyone was calling me Dolly. I listened closely
to any advice she offered.

"Try to just get used to the amount of time it takes for the salmon to reach medium rare. And learn the feel."

When she saw me comparing my closed fist to a piece of meat, pressing on the meaty part of my palm below the thumb with my fingers closed in a fist, she rolled her eyes.

"That's how they taught us at school," I said sheepishly. It was an old trick: Well done is a fist; rare is an open, relaxed hand. I hadn't been able to perform the trick back in school, either; I should have known better than to try it at work.

"Forget that," she said dismissively. "You don't have time to sit there and decide whether your lamb kebab feels like your stupid hand. Just get used to the *feeling*. Don't think so much."

The more hours I put in actually working as a cook, the more I realized how little practical knowledge I'd gained in cooking school. Meany and Jessie were patient with me while I regressed back to the land of insecurity. *Is this medium?* I would ask for a second opinion, holding a lamb kebab out for them to touch. *This is mid-rare, right?* pointing to a salmon. Well done was the only temp in which I had confidence (just cook it until it's too done to eat) but also the least likely to be ordered. Meany taught me how to use the different parts of the grill (the hottest spot in the center-right, the relatively cooler outer edges) to control my timing. After a while, I finally got the hang of it. I just touched. And felt. I had no other choice; the pace on the line on a busy night left me no time for thinking. I became a machine. Joey yelled out commands, and I executed them without emotional attachment—most of the time.

One busy night, Joey called out order after order as Layla's dining room filled up. When we were really busy, the new orders began to overlap with those that he'd already yelled out. *Three chicken, one sauce on the side; three lamb kebabs, all medium; five salmon—that makes seven salmon all day, three mid-rare, three medium, and one well done. Two swordfish kebabs. Three octo. Two merguez. Make that four chicken all day. Order fire!* He did us the favor of giving us the "all day" number, which included previously called orders, so we'd have the total number of orders that should be in the works. I could barely get the food out of the low-boy and onto sizzle platters before he started piling on more orders.

And he sounded uncharacteristically on edge. Maybe Drew, owner of the restaurant group of which we were a part, was in the restaurant. Drew had enough restaurants that he couldn't possibly spend every night at Layla, and since we had been open for over a year and had already received an excellent two-star review from the *New York Times,* he only stopped by occasionally. Though Joey was not an owner of the restaurant, he took full responsibility for its success or failure. His reputation as a chef was at stake. Still, he ultimately answered to Drew, who, as owner, had final say on any and all decisions. As far as I could tell, they had a good relationship and aside from insisting that kebabs be on the menu, Drew gave Joey the flexibility to run the restaurant the way Joey saw fit.

Drew was generally jovial and even willing to help out in the dining room during a rush. Still, when Drew came around (Heavy D. we lovingly called him, on account of his superior girth), everyone got a bit tense. He had an uncanny knack for face and name rec-ognition, which only made everyone more nervous; if we fucked something up, he'd remember forever. Until I actually saw Heavy D., though, I had no way of knowing if he was in the restaurant. And with all the orders Joey was yelling out, I was too busy to ask.

My grill quickly filled up and was wall-to-wall meat and fish. Joey just kept calling out more orders. *Add on another chicken and an octo.* Where was I supposed to cook all of it? Couldn't he see that my grill was full? I thought he was pushing me once again, testing me, on the busiest night I'd ever had. I became frustrated, and I let it show.

"Oh, *come on,*" I mumbled in exasperation, quietly but audibly.

I talked back. I complained. I questioned my chef, who heard me and then—worst of all—called me on it. In an instant I was horrified at my show of insubordination.

"Is there a problem," Joey said sternly and then paused before saying my name, "Dolly?" He had the tone of a reprimanding parent using an impetuous child's full name: *Is there a problem . . . Dalia Therese Jurgensen?*

"No, Joey," I answered, not turning around to face him, not stopping for a split second. "There's no problem."

Joey had the unique ability to discipline any employee with no more than a stern tone. It wasn't so much that we feared him; more that we feared disappointing him. We all wanted his ap-proval, and he knew it.

"How long on thirty-five, Dolly?" asked Jessie, saving me from further distraction.

She was referring to table thirty-five, whose order had been called what seemed like hours earlier. It was a four-top with two of the entrées coming off of my station: two grape leaf–wrapped salmon with chickpea pancakes and tahini vinaigrette, medium rare. It was a recent addition to the menu and one on which Meany and Jessie had collaborated. Joey liked their idea of wrapping salmon in grape leaves so much that he worked with them to create the full dish, making sure that it fit with the rest of the menu and still had his touch. He was secure enough in his own talents and abilities that he was ready and willing to teach and encourage his cooks to experiment with food, a trait sadly not always present in accomplished chefs.

That night, Jessie was working the sauté, or middle, station. She led the line, controlling the timing of the pickups, organizing the various entrées and tables so that everything went out in a controlled and timely fashion. She timed her entrées to be ready when mine and Meany's were (Meany was on hot app that night; as sous-chef she rotated through all the stations, covering other cooks' days off) and vice versa. I gently squeezed the sides of the two dark rectangles of salmon that were close to being done.

"One minute," I answered, moving the salmon to a sizzle platter so they could rest on the edge of the hot grill. Even away from direct heat, they would continue to cook, and by the time we picked up the table, the salmon would be perfect. I was thankful to free up a tiny bit of space on my grill.

Side towel in hand, I pulled down a stack of sauté pans from the top of the *sally,* short for salamander, the overhead broiler that ran a third of the length of the hot line. Always on, it provided the perfect hot spot to store pans and plates to keep them warm. After months of working on the hot line, my forearms had taken on a new shape as a result of the palm-up lift I used to retrieve an entire stack of sauté pans from the top of the sally. Meany, Jessie, and I often compared muscles, proudly flexing different parts of our arms and hands; no one could top Jessie's biceps. Catching sight of my own bulging forearms, a tangible symbol of my growing strength, was always satisfying, even in the midst of being slammed.

"Ready, Dolly?" asked Jessie without a break in her movement.

"Ready," I answered, anxious to clear the order for table thirty-five and focus on the monster pickup that was monopolizing my grill.

I moved the two salmon onto my cutting board and, side towel in hand, pulled down two dinner plates from the shelf that sat above the flattop (strategically placed to keep them warm). I may as well have had folded side towels surgically attached to my hands since I needed them to touch virtually everything on the hot line.

I set one of the chickpea pancakes, studded with small squares of tomato and chopped black olives and cooked in brown butter, in the center of each white plate. Now the salmon. With my sharpened chef knife (a sharp edge is absolutely imperative; you need to cut, not tear), I sliced each rectangle of fish on the bias with one smooth motion. Then, fingers proverbially crossed, I pulled the two halves of the salmon apart to check the color: perfect. The deep coral-colored center gradually gave way to the pale pink of the fully cooked outer edges of the fish. It didn't matter how long I'd worked on the grill, I always crossed my fingers before cutting open a salmon. If the salmon was too rare (which happened a lot in the beginning) I had to smoosh the cut sides back together and put the fish back in the oven on a sizzle platter to finish cooking, which never resulted in the perfectly graduated glow of color I was aiming for. At least once a week I had an anxiety dream in which, no matter what I did (even if I barely set it on the grill for a second), every salmon I cut open was well done—overcooked and useless. Garbage. It was only marginally better than my recurring stress dreams from garde-manger in which I woke up in bed with an enormous bowl of tabouleh on the pillow next to me.

But those salmon were perfect. I placed the two halves atop the chickpea pancake, showcasing the beautiful pinks, and spooned the tahini vinaigrette around the outside of the plate. A drizzle of deep brown veal sauce (an unlikely but delicious pairing) contrasted with the thick, sand-colored tahini and finished my work on the plate. Joey would put on the final touches: a tiny quenelle of thick yogurt and a salmon skin chip—the fishy version of a pork rind. As Jessie was putting the final touches on her roasted cod and pan-seared monkfish, we set our plates on the pass for Joey to finish, wipe clean, and hand off to a waiter. He barely looked at me as I passed him the plates. I hoped he'd forgotten my earlier grumbling.

With so much food to put out, more than I'd ever had at once, I didn't have time to worry about Joey. My grill overflowing, I had to access all the techniques and skills I'd been honing to get the food out. I needed to be "in the zone." I went into serious automatic pilot mode: I spun into action, arranging everything in the appropriate places on the grill. Anything well done went on the hottest spot, while swordfish kebabs that cooked more quickly stayed near the edges. Zaatar-spiced chicken took the longest, even though I had "marked" or par-cooked each portion at the beginning of service, so I put them on first. I had my own system to keep it all straight, so that the well-done salmon was finished at the same time as the medium lamb kebab and so on. I'm not even sure how I developed this system; I just did. I intuitively knew what was what.

I filled sauté pans with enough curried bulgur wheat and orzo salad for all the plates, and sautéed eggplant pancakes (reminiscent of latkes) for the chicken and chickpea pancakes for the salmon. As soon as the octopus legs were ready, I passed them down the line to the new garde-manger cook to get them out of my way. I grabbed a stack of plates and lined them up along both my counter and the small stainless steel edge that abutted the grill and flattop. My entire area was white with plates, with only hints of stainless steel peeking through between them. My heart was racing, Joey's reprimand a distant memory, quickly fading into the haze of steam and sweat and smoke. We all wore undershirts to soak up the perspiration, but also to protect us from the starchy roughness of the chef's jackets, and the amount of sweat running off me was astonishing.

"Dolly!" yelled Meany and Jessie in unison. Was it time already?

Tongs in one hand, sauté pan of bulgur wheat in the other, I glanced over at them. They had only four plates to pick up between them compared to my fourteen. They were staring absurdly at me, raising their arms and hands above their heads over and over again, grinning. What the hell?

"We're giving you the wave!" explained Jessie.

"You got a full grill, Dolly!" Meany added. "You get the wave."

Sopping with sweat, sauté pan in hand surrounded by a cloud of smoke, I giggled uncontrollably. Instantly, the tension was broken, so that a moment later when it was time to put up the food, I was fully prepared and at ease. Jessie and Meany helped me with my plates, and we three worked together while waiters lined up to pick up the finished plates after we passed them off to Joey.

The rush continued, but more evenly divided among our stations, until it began to dissipate. Finally, we got a brief reprieve as the flow of orders ebbed and the music came on. The wobbly Middle Eastern music filled the restaurant, and from the completely open kitchen we saw the delight of anticipation on the diners' faces. She came at the same time every night, entering just as most of the tables were relaxing into their entrées: the belly dancer.

She glided into the room, finger cymbals clinking to the music, filmy costume flowing around her, framing her bare belly and barely clad, full, shaking hips. When it was a Friday or Saturday night, it was only a matter of time before our two-star restaurant started to feel more like a bachelor party. Men in suits and ties suddenly felt compelled to stuff dollar bills into the belly dancer's skirt as they awkwardly tried to match her moves shimmy for shimmy, while she danced away, sword balanced on top of her head.

Jessie, Meany, and I looked at one another. We realized a long time ago that the rhythm of this particular music resembled the beat of another well-known dance. We got in line, one in front of the other. We stepped twice to the right. Twice to the left. Once forward. Once backward. Hop. Hop. Hop. Dressed in our dirty, baggy uniforms, robust sweat beads, and arms riddled with scars and blisters, we went unnoticed by the diners, the women who made the food they were enjoying, as we bunny hopped down our line. No one noticed, that is, except for Joey, who could not hide his smile.

After work, we changed back into our street clothes after trying in vain to wash some of the dirt and smell and grease off at least our hands and forearms. As was our routine, we headed over to the Rat Bar. If it had a real name, we didn't know it. It was not unusual to see rats running around in front of it, hence, the Rat Bar or, simply, the Rat. It was the closest bar, just a block away, with a bartender who knew us by name and was always happy to buy us a round.

Even more than I had at Nobu, I wholeheartedly embraced the late-night social scene. Cooking was more physically exhausting than plating desserts and, as a result, left me more wired. After a shift, we were worked up, and all we wanted was a drink, lots of drinks. After a few hours, maybe we'd want a snack, too, but mostly we wanted to drink.

Hunched around a small table at the Rat, we'd talk about the only thing all of us really had in common: cooking. More often than not, we'd rehash the ups and downs of that night's service: *Oh my God, Dolly, your grill was soooo jamming! HIGH FIVE! . . . Did you see that asshole trying to dirty-dance with the belly dancer? LOSER! . . . Juan, I never saw you roll dough so fast. Your face was covered in flour! HIGH FIVE!* We did a lot of high-fiving. Occasionally Joey joined us for an after-work drink. He was the king of high fives and would stand up from his chair and reach across the table just to make contact with someone on the other side.

Although all the various cooks at Layla (aside from Sprout, that is) got along, we were all insanely different people, and, for the most part, had we not been thrown together in that kitchen, I doubt that we would ever have spoken to one another, let alone become friends who spent every night hanging out. Kitchens have a funny way of forcing people, as different as they may be, to get along.

Juan was around my age—mid-twenties—from Puerto Rico, as gay as the day is long, and just as eager to talk about it, especially around anyone who would feel uncomfortable. *Chris,* he would say, as he snuggled up to the daytime sous-chef, a macho he-man type from New Jersey. Chris, who had a checkered past that included jail, drugs, and fights, liked women. He probably picked fights with people like Juan when he was a kid. *Chris, you won't believe it, but I had the best fist-fuck of my life last night,* Juan would taunt. At first, Chris would become visibly incensed, though he would keep his temper in check. After a while, he just laughed it off, and eventually they became friends—sort of. *Don't tell him this,* Chris told us, *but I'd kill anyone who tried to mess with Juan.*

When Sheila started, there was a lot of snickering and rumors that she was (gasp!) a lesbian. She was, but after a few weeks no one cared or snickered. Meany was born and raised in Queens, New York, and could be a tough Spanish-speaking grunt one minute and a lip-glossed sophisticated food person the next. Soft-spoken and subtle Jessie, who came from Virginia, had a silly sense of humor (she would hold a long, stiff, translucent sheet of dried salmon skin under her nose as a mustache or under her chin as a bow tie). And then there was me, a Jersey girl fresh out of culinary school. I had so badly wanted to be a chef, but after a year cooking at Layla, I was, quite sadly, realizing that maybe I had been wrong.

There was so much I loved: the chopping, the preparing, the actual cooking. I even loved the heat and the sweat of it all. I loved the camaraderie, the way we all worked together, and how each one of us brought something, literally and figuratively, to the table. But it was hard. We worked six days a week, for ten or more hours a day. Getting two days off in a row was a possibility, but it meant working thirteen days straight. The restaurant never closed, ever. In that year I rarely saw my family or any friends from my former life. I was unable to see friends that came into town, support friends' performances in bands or plays, even go out to dinner, unless it happened after midnight. Even if I could take an extra day off, it would be unpaid, and earning only $425 a week, a mere $25 more than I'd made at Nobu, I simply could not afford any extra days off. I was still paying for my own health insurance because, of course, the restaurant did not provide it for their nonmanagement employees (cooks and waiters). And because of the nature of restaurants (one person per station per night), calling in sick was next to impossible; who would grill my chicken if I didn't come in? Everyone else would be busy doing something else. Personal days? Yeah, right.

None of these frustrations were considered valid grounds for complaint, because though restaurant kitchens allow people to be themselves, whatever form that may take (and it is still my over-whelmingly favorite thing about restaurant kitchens), they do not allow for complaints of any kind. Joey, fair as he was with his staff, was of the school that considered the long hours, poor pay, and lack of health insurance simply part of the job. If you couldn't take it, well, then you were weak and in the wrong business. After a year, I began to feel like maybe I couldn't take it. Maybe I was weak.

My time at Layla also gave me the opportunity to see what be-ing a chef is really all about. It wasn't the actual cooking—the seasoning, the techniques, the knowledge—that intimidated me; I felt pretty confident that I could eventually master all of those things. It was all the other stuff I hadn't thought about; being able to cook good food was only half of the job. Joey had to oversee not only a staff of cooks but also dishwashers and prep cooks, and he had to be on top of all the waiters as well. He was a master at handling the endless variety of personalities that end up in a res-taurant and getting everyone to do as he wanted the way that he wanted. He had to discipline anyone who stepped out of line or slacked off, and he had to make sure the purveyors weren't cheat-ing him. He had to be in charge (of personnel, of food, of bud-gets) while simultaneously charming the press, the customers, sometimes even Heavy D. Joey was supremely confident and commanded ultimate authority, two characteristics that had just not made it into my DNA.

But maybe I was just down on myself. Maybe over time I would develop these skills. Maybe all I needed, really, was a break.

TEN

✦

Takeout

Joey wasn't that surprised when I gave him my notice.

"I think I just need a break," I told him. What else could I say? It wasn't like I'd found another job. I wasn't actually sure what I was going to do.

"Well, Doll," he said. "I'm sorry to see you go, but I know you haven't been too happy recently."

"It's not that I'm not happy . . ." I wanted to explain, but I feared that anything I said would offend him and I definitely didn't want to offend Joey.

"So, what are you gonna do?" he asked, ignoring my lame response.

"I don't know," I told him. It was true, but why did I always feel like such an idiot talking to Joey? It was easier to communicate over order-fires; he told me what to do and I did it. "Maybe try food styling?" As if he would remember a comment he'd made almost a year ago.

"Well," he went on, ignoring my attempt at a half joke, "I know a guy who has a catering business. He could probably use you a few days a week, here and there. Pays pretty good. Tell him I sent you."

After a brief phone conversation, Joey's friend Bob gave me an address on Twenty-fourth Street and told me to meet him on the eleventh floor, wearing chef's pants.

The address was the service entrance to an office building. I walked out of the elevator into a gray hallway, where two guys in chef's coats and black-and-white-checked pants were hunched over a long table.

Bob looked up. "Dolly?" I couldn't believe Joey actually told him my name was Dolly.

At the end of the table, there was a waist-high metal cart filled with sheet pans, each one lined with food, some of it bite-sized, some of it still needing to be cut. The table was set up with cutting boards and littered with knives, crumbs, and silver trays. People dressed in black pants and white shirts randomly opened the door to the hallway, letting in the hum of office party chatter, to pick up a tray filled with hors d'oeuvres. Cater waiters.

"So," Bob explained, handing me a chef's coat. "We've got about twenty different hors d'oeuvres here for this party, some sort of work anniversary or something. Joey said you had pastry experience."

I nodded.

"That's excellent. I'm gonna have you cut this napoleon." He pointed to a large rectangle: three sheets of puff pastry layered with smoked salmon mousse and chive goat cheese. He handed me a long serrated knife. "Just cut them into bite-sized squares, like this." He pointed to a tray of hors d'oeuvres. "Then you can arrange them on a silver tray."

I cut the napoleon into small, even squares, then moved on to some of the other, less messy hors d'oeuvres. The top shelf of the metal cart was reserved for hot hors d'oeuvres, which we heated with cans of Sterno lit just below it. Mini crab cakes, mini goat cheesecakes crusted with almonds, marinated shrimp, all had been cooked back at the caterer's kitchen, and we just warmed them up, adding a garnish before sending them out.

I treated the area just as I would any kitchen station. I organized everything as efficiently and neatly as possible. At the end of the party, we cleaned off the table, threw out any leftover food, and restocked the rolling cart with dirty stuff to bring back to the catering kitchen.

"So," Bob said as we loaded everything back into his van on the street. "I'd like to use you again. We pay seventeen dollars an hour, and you can work as many or as few days as you'd like."

Seventeen dollars an hour! I quickly calculated that I could work just fewer than thirty hours a week and make the same money I made at Layla. And from what I could tell, it wasn't that difficult a job. No flaming grills, no one yelling for ten plates at a time. I began my stint as a freelance catering cook.

On my next day of work, I helped prepare the food for an upcoming event and arrived ready to scoop out hundreds of crab cakes or peel piles of carrots. Kevin, the head chef of the company, showed me around the kitchen, which had most of the same equipment as any restaurant but with lots more preparation and storage space.

"You have pastry experience, right?" he asked. Again with the pastry experience. I didn't yet realize what a commodity it was.

"Yes," I answered.

"Excellent," he told me. "You can start by rolling out these sheets of puff pastry. We need them about double the size they are now, about an eighth of an inch thick."

"Okay," I said, looking at the two boxes full of puff pastry sheets. Rolling out puff pastry was tricky, mostly because it had to be partially frozen, or at least quite cold, while rolling. If it got too warm, it would just snap back to its smaller size. And it had to be rolled evenly, otherwise it wouldn't puff properly when baked. It was a tedious task and, I was sure, a test. If I passed (rolled out the dough adequately and quickly enough, and didn't complain), I would be given better tasks and be asked to work more often.

For six months I lived the life of a freelance caterer. Just as Bob had promised, I was able to work as much or as little as I wanted. If I wanted to go to a friend's party one Friday night, I simply told Bob I was unavailable, and, without asking questions or giving me any guilt, he simply found someone else. If I wanted to make a little extra cash, I signed up for as many parties as possible, of which there was rarely a shortage.

We did small private parties in people's homes, which more often than not left me envious. I could not believe the size and utter grandeur of some of these New York City apartments. This other half always had the most amazing kitchens in their homes, yet they got little use, except for when we arrived, drooling over the multitude of All-Clad pots and pans, the high-end machinery and refrigeration. The irony was always lost on the client.

We did a lot of business events, too: cocktail parties, fundraisers, corporate promotions, sit-down dinners, sometimes for up to fifteen hundred guests. I learned how to plate food for hundreds of guests at a time and to "cook" food with nothing more than small tubs of the glowing gelatinous goo called Sterno.

Soon, I was able to "run" small parties (usually in private homes), which meant being the head kitchen person, taking full responsibility for all the food, and earning $25 an hour. It also meant dealing with the client/host, and although some of them were sincerely thankful for my efforts, others treated me more like a servant than a trained professional.

My fellow cooks were always rotating and represented a wide range of cooking backgrounds. Some, like me, had come from high-end restaurants and just needed a break or were simply between jobs; others made virtual careers out of freelancing and even did small side jobs on their own. Kevin, the head chef of the catering company, had already been a chef in his own right but left the restaurant world in search of a more sane lifestyle, one with less pressure, fewer hours, and more money. He planned on returning to restaurants one day and resented the oft-heard sentiment that cooks who trade in the restaurant world for jobs in catering, private clubs, or corporate dining are cooks who simply can't hack it in the restaurant world.

I liked the freedom, the money, even the variety of the foods we prepared—for a while, but where was I going? I didn't have enough experience to become a head catering chef. My life as a freelance cook didn't offer much in the way of stability, either. I realized that, as much as it had worn me out, restaurant life offered a steady camaraderie and an environment in which I learned something, really learned something, because I had to do it over and over and over again, every day. Every task I did at Layla and Nobu—every dish, every vinaigrette, cookie, and sauce—I remembered. They had seeped into my skin. And in restaurants, I had worked closely with a chef, almost as an apprentice, and I missed that kind of guidance.

When a fellow catering cook mentioned he had a friend who was looking for pastry people, my interest was piqued. When he told me the restaurant was La Côte Basque, a venerable three-star restaurant practically legendary for the large number of ultimately famous chefs who had passed through its kitchens, I was even more interested. If I was going to return to restaurants, it had to be to a respected one. And I didn't mind that it was a pastry job; if I had learned anything from working in catering, it was that having pastry experience was a commodity, something that a lot of chefs and cooks either didn't know that much about or simply didn't have that much interest in. And, unlike a savory chef, pastry chefs have smaller staffs, smaller menus, and fewer budgetary concerns. With more experience under my belt and a different perspective because of it, pastry chef started to seem like it might be a good fit, definitely a path worth looking into. My six-month catering stint had given me just the break I needed.

ELEVEN

✦

French 101

I should have known that something was a bit off when the new pastry chef of La Côte Basque chose a bar on Sixth Avenue for our first meeting and interview. He had not officially started work at the restaurant yet and had to find an alternative meeting place. At least that's what he said. He told me to just look for a guy wearing a French soccer shirt. He bought me a beer, and I gave him my résumé, a fair trade, I guess, for my time, though he barely glanced at my résumé.

"The job is five days a week," he said in a mild French accent, "and pays six hundred and fifty dollars a week."

He must have been in his early forties. His dirty-blond hair was longish and beginning to thin—not a good combination. He had worked in plenty of restaurants I had heard of though never eaten at and had trained and worked extensively in France before coming to New York. I knew that French training was rigorous and exceptional; he had to know his stuff. He hardly asked me any questions at all and didn't even ask me to trail before offering me the job. I thought I'd hit the restaurant job jackpot.

The pastry kitchen at La Côte Basque was amazing (pastry had its own mini kitchen, not just a table squished into a crowded room like at Nobu and Layla). We were segregated (in the best possible sense) into a corner of the large basement prep area, with our own set of double-decker convection ovens, a six-top burner, a total of ten reach-in refrigerators, and five reach-in freezers. One of our six-foot prep tables was covered in a thick slab of marble, the perfect cool surface for working with doughs and chocolate. We had three industrial mixers, from a twelve-quart all the way up to one with a bowl so enormous I could easily have bathed in it. There was even a sheeter, a machine that quickly rolls out dough to exact thicknesses.

The new pastry chef quickly began changing the enormous dessert menu. There were twelve items in all, and since the restaurant was prix fixe, everyone got dessert, which meant we were very busy. But, though his technical abilities were clearly exceptional, I was disappointed in his aesthetic, which seemed dated and stale. Worst of all, his desserts just weren't things I'd want to eat. I cringed every time I had to plate his warm apple tarte Tatin with green apple sorbet. Sorbet on a warm dessert? I imagined the sorbet melting into a watery pool as it arrived at the table, rendering the dessert a soggy, one-note, green apple mess—disgusting. And

I hated the monstrously large vanilla tuiles I made to go with his *vacherin* (a classic French dessert consisting of baked meringue, ice cream, and whipped cream). The grossly jagged triangles stood nearly eight inches high and often sagged in the summer humidity, if the awkward cookies didn't break first. It was as though he designed desserts using only his head, without giving enough thought to what they actually tasted like or how they would be received by the average diner. It was a sad realization: Even highly skilled people can have bad taste. I really had become a dessert snob.

Most of all, though, I was disappointed by the pastry chef's lack of enthusiasm. He went through the motions of being a pastry chef, as if it were routine and rote. I was eager to learn, and he, it seemed, just wanted to pick up his paycheck.

When I had time at night, after the pastry chef had gone home, I would stand at the edge of the savory kitchen upstairs, watching Chef, the legendary owner and a forty-plus-year veteran of cooking, at the reins of his team of unwieldy line cooks. *Two canard, asshole, two!! Three chicken!* He would bellow out the orders into a microphone, and the cooks would move, as fast and furiously as they could, to meet his demands and avoid his wrath. Chef deemed cooks and waiters "assholes" when they'd done something wrong; the rest of the time, he simply referred to them generically as "François." All of them François, regardless of their given names or position. Still, I envied the excitement up there, their devotion to the craft. Where was my leader? My teacher?

Hope arrived when I learned that the pastry chef had also failed to impress Chef. The silver-haired Chef occasionally noticed me standing enviously on the sidelines of his kitchen, and one night he came over to me. *Don't worry, ma petite,* he said, *I'm going to find a new chef de pâtisserie.* He took the black Sharpie marker tucked into my collar and drew a heart just below my left shoulder. *Just be patient.* As he replaced the marker in my collar I saw one of the cooks roll his eyes. Chef had been yelling at them all night, calling them "asshole," and here he was drawing hearts on my chef's coat while I just stood there doing nothing.

Encouraged by Chef's promise of a new pastry chef, I tried to be patient. Every day when I came to work, the familiar smell of raw meat, vegetable scraps, and leaking garbage juices hit me as soon as I was buzzed in through the service entrance. Halfway down the hall, I prepared myself for a distinct shift in odor while passing a small room that consisted of a single, yellow-stained urinal containing an ineffective puck of disinfectant floating in a permanent puddle of unflushed pee, and a small stall guarded by a door that didn't shut properly: the employee bathroom. I tried to ignore the brown-smudged toilet paper snowballs that continued to litter the floor despite desperate handwritten notices: *Put your paper in the toilet and flush them after you wipe your ass!*

Then, it was on to the uniform shelf, where I began my futile search for a pair of regulation black-and-white-checked pants that would fit me. Having the restaurant supply our uniform was meant to be a perk that relieved us of the cost of buying our own sets and of laundering them: jackets (expensive on a cook's salary) can be worn only one time before being washed, and cooks have no desire to spend their precious time off doing extra laundry. Accordingly, pants might be stretched to last two or three days. If

I was lucky, I would find a size thirty and only have to roll the waist over once in order to keep them from falling down, but I was only this lucky about half of the time. I wished I could wear the colorful, elastic-waist pants I'd worn at Nobu, but La Côte Basque was old school, and *everyone* wore the standard issue man-pants. I didn't want to draw any additional attention to myself; I was already the only woman in the kitchen. I quietly resigned myself to the oversized pants and jackets.

I changed in a dusty storage room that was cluttered with every-thing from roasting pans to boxes of doilies to cases of cooking wine. It also doubled as the preferred break room for a group of butchers and prep guys, the only group, in fact, that actually took proper breaks every day at precisely the same time I started my shift. Like a high school clique, they stuck together, and they took up any remaining space in my "locker room," using sacks of dirty linen as beanbag chairs.

"*Hola, blanquita!*" They always greeted me this way.

It was bad enough that they didn't use (or even know) my real name, but did they have to call me White Girl? And with such gusto? It was the only time they talked to me at all.

"*Hola,*" I answered indifferently. Sometimes, I would notice an open bottle of cooking wine stashed behind one of their beanbags.

"Are you guys almost finished?" I would ask. "You know I have to change."

They might look at each other with amusement, but nobody would move. My five foot, two inch, 110-pound female frame did little to intimidate them. God forbid they do me the slightest of favors for fear of appearing to have given in to the authority of a woman.

I would grab my clogs from my locker, a makeshift wooden cubby, and head to a musty back corner of the room, where I would quickly rearrange some paper towel boxes and a few stacks of sauté pans. Then I would drape an extra chef's coat over a spare coatrack so I would be partially protected from their view or at least my midsection would. The illusion of privacy was better than none.

In La Côte Basque I found the stereotypical restaurant I'd been warned about in culinary school. It was dominated by men, and for most of my time there, I was the only woman on the premises, aside from a coat-check woman who was relegated to a closet upstairs beside the dining room. I had been warned about chauvinism in the restaurant world, but, call me naïve, call me a product of my Danish parents' egalitarian upbringing, it had not actually occurred to me that I might one day have to face it.

The masculine and outsized uniforms I had to wear and the daily ignoring of my simple request for privacy while changing were just the beginning. Sexist comments became so frequent that it was almost comical. There was the new, older cook in his forties who, after his first night working in the kitchen, declared, *Man, that kitchen is hot! There's no way a chick could take that heat . . . unless maybe she's a dyke.* I didn't bother telling him about the bunny-hopping hot line at Layla. He, of course, didn't last more than a few weeks. (Sad but true, most cooks who start later than their twenties simply don't make it.) Then there was the prep cook who cornered me any time he could to rasp lasciviously, *Tienes novio?* My lies about my long-term, very big boyfriend did little to dissuade him.

The waiters turned out to be the worst offenders. Mostly well into their late fifties and even sixties, they "innocently" offered me stays at their summerhouses, while they nonchalantly curled an arm around my twenty-six-year-old figure. The younger ones were even worse, reprimanding my every bite of chocolate, bread and butter, or candy: *Don't get fa-at!* they would condescend in a singsong voice. If I ever talked back to them or, worse, ordered them to please not eat the petits fours off the already assembled plates, their response was always the same: *What's the matter? Got your period?* Even the local labor union that represented the restaurant workers (weren't they supposed to maintain respect for and protect the equality of those in the workplace?) let me down. *Dear Sir,* the letter began. That a woman might work in the kitchen simply didn't occur to them, I guess.

If I learned anything from working in a sea of men who had little regard or respect for the job I did, it was that I had no recourse. Reasoning was futile. Had I expressed my indignation, I would have been regarded as "typical," or, even worse, I would have been labeled a "bitch." Making enemies would only have made my daily life, already barely tolerable, that much more difficult. I would never be physically stronger than they were, nor did I have any chance of growing a penis or beating them at their own game. No, the only way I could win—or even just tie—was to not be beaten, to not allow them to prevent me from doing my job. I could work harder and faster and better. In the meantime, I crossed my fingers for a new pastry chef.

Glen came in like a whirlwind, fresh from an extended trip working in France and ready to take control of La Côte Basque's pastry department. He was mid-thirties at most, tall and lean, with a face much younger than his years, and a boyish haircut to match. Most important, he was supremely dedicated to the success of his desserts and his career. He brought with him a red metal toolbox on wheels that stood as high as my shoulders and required two guys to carry down the stairs. Each drawer was filled with different pastry tools: one with spatulas, one with stencils, one with knives, another with decorating combs. One drawer held different sets of recipes (creams, cakes, petits fours), a lot of them from his recent stint in France. Most chefs I'd known up to that point kept their tools in toolboxes but the variety with a single handle and a tray, with some storage underneath. Glen's box was incredible, and, from the looks of it, brand new. That toolbox made quite an impression.

Eager to show off his talent and ability, and determined to prove himself, Glen jumped right in, changing much of the menu at once. He was disgusted to find that the menu's Seasonal Fruit Tart, a mainstay of the restaurant, was a ten-inch tart sliced to order. *What is this? A diner?* He immediately mandated thoroughly modern-looking individual fruit tarts, assembled with seasonal fruit and pastry cream, made fresh every day by Sega, a pastry cook, and served with grapefruit sorbet made from juice we squeezed ourselves. And when he saw the apple tarte Tatin with green apple sorbet, he was as horrified as I'd been. His mantra, which he bellowed forcefully and often, was: It's all about the flavor. *Taste it!* he'd urge, pushing a new item in my face. *It's all about the flavor.*

I was instantly intrigued by his style and techniques, especially with chocolate. He made hundreds of chocolate bonbons at a time, layering colored cocoa butter and different kinds of chocolate to create miniature edible pieces of art. He even turned the most ordinary dessert—ice cream—into a visual masterpiece by using chocolate garnishes: four small round scoops of ice cream or sorbet rested on a hovering painter's palette made out of chocolate that he'd given a wood-grain effect. The plate was complete with chocolate paintbrushes and a small easel that displayed individual modern artwork, all made out of chocolate. He was just the pastry chef I'd been hoping for. I even forgave him for reinstating the six-day work week with no increase in my pay. But getting used to the new desserts proved easier than getting used to Glen's big personality.

I learned to judge his mood upon my arrival. If he was feeling calm, it might be a great shift: He'd have the patience to teach me things and answer my questions. Maybe he'd be excited about some new ingredient he discovered or a new brand of chocolate. He often shoved things in my face. *I don't care if you don't like white chocolate,* he'd say, *just eat it! Let it melt in your mouth. . . . Amazing, right? Not too sweet.* At his worst, Glen could be grumpy and agitated, set off by the tiniest thing. He once hollered at me for having the hiccups. *Would you stop that fucking racket! I can't fucking take it anymore!* On those days I tried to stay out of his way.

Regardless of his mood, Glen littered our conversation, which became more social over time with his sometimes sketchy comments on current events and detailed personal stories that were not interesting to anyone but him.

"Hey," he said one day as I started work. He didn't look up from the paint sprayer he was cleaning. I could tell by the protective black garbage bags still draped in the corner that he'd just finished spraying the chocolate mousse domes he'd recently added to the menu. Every time we lined the corner with the black shiny bags, Glen said it reminded him of a porn set.

"You'll never believe what happened to me this morning," he said.

"Tell me," I said noncommittally. As if he needed encouragement.

"*Unbelievable!*" He put down the sprayer and looked at me. "I was walking to work this morning, and you know how windy it was, right?"

He didn't wait for my affirmation.

"So windy! And there was this *hot* girl waiting for the bus. She was wearing a skirt, you know, the flouncy kind. Just standing there. And this big gust of wind comes in and *whoosh!*" He flung his arms up in the air over his head. "Her skirt flies up to her neck!"

"That's really exciting, Glen," I said.

"No, you don't get it. That's not all." He paused and looked at me urgently, making sure I understood the significance of what he was about to say. "She was wearing a *thong!*" he yelled with all the triumph of a twelve-year-old boy. "Her whole ass was completely bare!"

"Wow," I said flatly. "You're really lucky."

"Yeah," he said, nodding. "I know."

I didn't really mind Glen's stories; in fact, I usually found them kind of funny. Actually what was really funny was his telling them to me. The idea that getting a sneak peek of a stranger's butt could excite him so much was far more laughable than the story itself. I could handle a few stupid stories and inappropriate comments; at least he respected the job I was doing. Plus, his desserts were amazing, and he was willing to teach me everything. With Glen's help, I grew by leaps and bounds.

Glen showed me how to melt together the right proportions of cocoa butter and chocolate (a ratio of 1:1) to get a liquid that would spew evenly out of the paint sprayer. Sprayed onto something cold, like frozen chocolate mousse domes, the spray would instantly bead up upon hitting the cold surfaces, giving them a rough, sandpaperlike look. Used on something room temperature, the spray remained glossy and smooth, like paint.

It was Glen who turned me onto secret centers—surprise flavors and textures hidden at the center of a dessert. Each chocolate mousse dome had a miniature crème brûlée hiding in its middle. And instead of saucing the plate for his *fromage blanc* mousse cake, he froze the raspberry sauce into small discs and then stuffed them inside the cakes before the mousse was fully set. Diners would discover the now-melted sauce, trapped inside the cheesecake, upon digging into the dessert.

He had fun with his aesthetic, too. His cheesecake was wrapped in a thin band of dense sponge cake that was decorated with bright, swirling colors, each one reminiscent of a wild, otherworldly sunset. He piped chocolate sorbet into small tubular molds that he then froze overnight so that each of his orange crème brûlée tarts had a cylinder of sorbet next to it, standing tall, rather than just a plain old scoop. Over time, his personality grew on me, too.

He seemed to enjoy my absolute disinterest in any of his attempts to astonish or impress me. Had we not ended up in the same kitchen, we would surely never have had the occasion even to speak to each other, our personalities were so different. Nevertheless, we became unlikely partners in pastry with a vaguely symbiotic relationship: I needed (and wanted) his expertise; he needed me to tolerate his prepubescent stories, political harangues, and moods. He depended on me to help him run the pastry department, too.

But after almost a year of working for Glen, I began to feel the familiar twinges of burnout. Maybe it was the six-day work week and long hours. Maybe it was Glen's erratic personality or his seemingly endless amounts of energy that I simply couldn't match. Or a combination of all these things, I suppose.

A friend, Robyn, had been getting steady work with *Martha Stewart Living,* both the magazine and television show, decorating cakes, developing recipes and ideas, and generally helping out in the test kitchen. I practically drooled when she told me her day rate. In three days she made nearly what I earned working six at La Côte Basque, minus the insulting and sexist comments, I was sure. Maybe it was the path for me. Joey *had* said I had a good eye. Robyn recommended me for a trail, and on my one day off, I took a train to Westport, Connecticut.

✦

TWELVE

In the Kitchen with Martha

I had not been a stalwart follower of Martha (like Oprah, she needed only one name), but I recognized her signature style the moment I walked into Martha Stewart Living Television for my trail. Everything looked effortlessly organized and decorated, from the walls and desks to the well-groomed and varied grounds, with most things painted in colors that had become associated with Martha. Even the light was soft and flattering.

But nothing could beat the test kitchen. It was equipped with a full-size walk-in refrigerator, deep stainless steel sinks, a wall of tall Sub-Zero freezers and restaurant-quality stoves, and standard stainless steel prep tables. At the same time, the kitchen looked like someone's (presumably Martha's) home kitchen. The walls were lined with white shelves, cupboards, and drawers, each one impeccably organized and marked with laser-printed black-and-white labels: knives, serving spoons, measuring spoons, bowls. Touches of trademark pale green peeked out between various drawers and shelves. Every single thing had its place and a label—a near impossibility in a restaurant, where equipment is more often shoved into a bin in a tangle of wire whisks, spatulas, and ladles.

I waved to my friend Robyn, who stood at a table quietly kneading dough as she chatted to another young woman who was leaning over a sheet of paper, taking notes. She smiled back. Everything seemed so calm, so pleasant. The kitchen even had a wall of windows that overlooked a meticulously tended garden. All of the palpable urgency and testosterone that prevailed so obviously in a restaurant kitchen simply did not exist here. It was like kitchen Valhalla. How hard could this trail be?

"We are the only national food show on a major network," Savannah, the kitchen director, said, politely impressing upon me the prestige of the show. She had a kind face: soft and round, with bright blue eyes. She always—always—said "please" and "thank you" and "ma'am," blanketing every syllable in a rich and sweet southern drawl. Most of the chefs I'd known so far were dead set on instant intimidation, but not Savannah. I knew from Robyn, who had quickly become one of her fans, that Savannah knew her stuff, and she knew food. This was a different world: She didn't need to intimidate or scream and yell to get respect; she simply earned it, and as kitchen director, she held my fate in her hands. She handed me a chocolate macaroon recipe and instructed me to alter the cookie in three distinctly different ways.

Robyn had told me I'd be given such a task, one that would measure how well I could manipulate recipes and develop ideas, which was a large part of the freelancer's job. Because the show aired daily, there was an endless need for new food segment ideas and original recipes. So, though we might comb through cookbooks to get basic ingredients and proportions for a given recipe, that was only a starting point. The recipe would go through trial after trial, with each change noted and tracked until the perfect recipe and finished product were achieved and approved by Martha herself. I had to pass the macaroon challenge.

I didn't wear a chef's coat; no one did. Instead, I just tied a long white apron around my waist and rolled up my sleeves. I pulled back my long hair, dyed near-white with black stripes (people working in restaurant kitchens are usually allowed a certain amount of freedom with their appearance that I, like Jemal, reveled in), and tucked my black-rimmed glasses into the collar of my shirt. I'd worn the glasses in an attempt to look a bit older, more serious. People often underestimated my age and thus, I feared, my ability.

I looked at the recipe and thought of different ways it could be changed: nuts could be added, or flavored extracts. They could be dipped in chocolate after cooling. Maybe they could be spread out on a sheet, the recipe tweaked, and reinvented as a bar cookie. Probably I could cut down the amount of sugar or substitute brown sugar for white. I got started measuring out ingredients using standard cups and spoons. Unlike restaurant recipes, which were almost always weighed out in grams (if there was a recipe at all), all of MSLTV recipes had to be accessible to the home cook. What use was making something on TV if a home viewer couldn't then make it herself?

Batch by batch, I baked different macaroon varieties, trying to remain organized and cleaning along the way, valuable work habits in any kitchen. From time to time, Robyn looked over her shoulder to make sure I was okay, and when I had questions everyone was eager to help. It was the quietest and most civilized day I ever spent working in a kitchen. Not a single profanity was uttered. I started dreaming about the calm and female-friendly work life that was so close at hand. No more sexual comments, no more oversized men's uniforms. No more working weekends.

When Savannah asked me to get cleaned up so we could talk, I reached into the collar of my shirt to retrieve my glasses. But my glasses were gone.

"Wait," I blurted to Savannah, who stood waiting for me to follow her onto the set where we would have privacy, "I lost my glasses." She just looked at me; she didn't care if I'd lost my glasses. I should have known better than to try using a prop. I tried to retrace my steps.

Suddenly, I knew with absolute certainty where they were. I did not slip them into my bag as I should have, nor had they fallen into the trash or onto the floor. I walked over to the oven I'd been using to bake my cookies and opened the oven door. There they were, resting in the fold of the oven door, warm and fatally warped.

Savannah and I sat in one of two unused darkened kitchen sets where Martha filmed the food segments, and, amazingly, she offered me three steady days of freelance work a week. Once again, I said good-bye to the restaurant world.

Glen did not congratulate me on my latest career move, but he accepted it, and after giving him two weeks' notice, I embarked on my new life as a part-time test kitchen freelancer. Three days a week, I took a train to Westport, Connecticut. My commute to the self-contained "compound," as we called it, was more than two hours door to door. I looked forward to using my time on this reverse commute to catch up on the reading I never seemed to have the time or energy for while working in a restaurant.

At first, I was given simple tasks, like shopping, which should have been brainless and easy. But rumors of Martha's perfectionism paralyzed me. I knew that nothing got by her and that she held everyone and everything up to her incredibly high standards. I'd heard more than one story that ended with someone crying— and it wasn't Martha. I would drive one of the company vans to the local store, shopping list in hand, and if Idaho potatoes were on the list, I would end up staring blankly at the bins of potatoes, suddenly second-guessing myself: *Are these Idaho?* I worried that the mangoes I chose wouldn't be ripe enough, that the grapes came from the wrong country, that I'd mistaken Napa cabbage for Savoy.

By the time I finally met Martha, my expectations had become so high that it felt anticlimactic. She marched into the test kitchen where I was working, remarked on the exhaust fans, looked at me as if I'd done something wrong, and then paused, as if suddenly realizing that a stranger was in her house.

"Ma'am, this is Dalia, our new freelancer," Savannah said, stepping forward. "She worked at Nobu." Savannah thought my experience at Nobu, a restaurant Martha liked, would help endear me to her. It didn't seem to. Martha simply nodded in my direction and walked out of the kitchen. At least she hadn't made me cry, but then again why should she? Her demands were no more challenging than those of any top chef. I had already worked with some pretty difficult chefs, and my thick skin had remained firmly in place. In fact, I respected her for demanding absolute quality and accepting nothing less. I could only guess that the rest of her staff, those who worked at desks beyond the confines of the test kitchen, were less accustomed to an occasionally gruff boss who, like a chef, had little patience for "feelings."

Once I started to relax, I loved shopping detail. I was getting *paid* to go to the grocery store and pick out the finest ingredients, something I did for fun at home or to pull myself out of a dull mood. And when I wasn't shopping, I was working in a gorgeous kitchen, using the finest ingredients and equipment with Robyn and Savannah, who were quickly becoming friends.

We were free to experiment with different foods, to *cook* without the pressure of a dining room full of hungry customers waiting to be served. On any given day we might try to come up with the perfect picnic lunch, the perfect chicken salad, the perfect lemon cake. We had a camaraderie, the three of us, bonding mostly over our love for cooking and, more important, eating, and working toward a common goal: coming up with ideas and recipes that would please Martha. Our only guideline was that anything we used to produce a dish had to be available—at least by mail order or via the Internet—to the average viewer. Martha insisted on it.

Quality ingredients were important, and whenever possible they came directly from Martha's property. We used eggs from her own chickens, which lived at her Westport home. The free-range, totally organic eggs were delivered by one of her helpers. We stored the blue, green, and brown eggs (even the eggs came in quintessential Martha colors—we were sure she chose chicken breeds based on their egg color) in large bowls in the walk-in. We set aside most of our food waste to be used as chicken feed and were careful to follow this rule. It was not beyond Martha to peek into our garbage cans to make sure we had not wasted any chicken food. Conversely, she would occasionally check the chicken food to make sure we hadn't carelessly given them something harmful, like a rubber band. The colorful eggs made beautiful props for the set, and their flavor was a revelation. The yolks were a bright yellow verging on neon, and their taste was exceptionally creamy and rich. When they were in excess, we eagerly scrambled them up as a snack.

But it wasn't just the eggs. Everything that Martha had on the show was authentic. Any edible props on the two sets were made in the test kitchen. The "mud room" off of one kitchen set was lined with shelves of jam made in the test kitchen, often with fruit that had come from one of Martha's properties. Why would we make jam from store- or even farm-bought fruit when there were blueberry bushes right outside? One gorgeous summer day we spent hours picking blueberries off the bushes that lined the front of the building. Martha's show was nothing if not authentic, and I was happy to work toward her goal of keeping it that way. No wonder she had so many adoring fans.

Picking blueberries, making jam, and scrambling fresh eggs with women I called my friends hardly seemed like work, but not all my days working for Martha were blissful. In fact, attempts to come up with yet another cookie to meet Martha's standards could be torture. Things we proudly presented to her could be shot down with little explanation, and we'd be forced back into the kitchen to meet a deadline.

And the days on which we recorded the food segments could be long, tedious, and exhausting. If we'd created the recipes for a segment, preparation for the taping was always easier; we were familiar with the recipes and could easily prepare them in their various stages. But when the recipes came from a guest chef, we needed plenty of time to test and tweak the recipes because, almost without exception, restaurant chefs—who prepare everything using taste and intuition (rather than measuring cups) and in large quantities—sent us inaccurate recipes. We reworked (and reworked) their recipes using standard kitchen tools and measures, ensuring that viewers would be able to re-create the dish based on the recipe used on the show. One famed pastry chef sent a recipe that simply did not work, no matter how often we attempted to prepare it. It just didn't make sense; pastry chefs are the ones who actually use their own recipes. He insisted time and time again that it was fine. We finally came to the conclusion that he'd done it on purpose to protect his spectacular French macaroons or his overblown ego.

Each segment (normally one dish per segment) had a designated cart on which we laid out everything Martha needed to execute the dish. Each ingredient sat in a different bowl, always with options so she could decide for herself at the last minute how to carry on. We also provided different forms of a given ingredient for use as a prop. If a recipe called for one-half cup of grated cheese, we included a hunk of the cheese (with the exact brand or producer, too, noted on a sheet of paper beside it), a grater, a measuring cup, and one-half cup of grated cheese in a bowl. We anticipated her every possible need and whim because nothing was worse than having Martha stop, mid-taping, to say, *I need to grate the cheese myself. Why don't I have a hunk of cheese?* Thankfully, the props department was responsible for color coordinating the bowls, towels, and serving plates.

Generally, the only time I saw Martha was on taping days, as she was too busy tending to her varied successful businesses—magazine, website, catalogue, books—to spend that much time in our kitchen. It crushed the dreams of my friends who had visions of Martha standing over the oven right by my side, gently holding a wooden spoonful of sauce to my mouth for a taste. But on taping days, Martha was "in the house," as we used to say, and her presence was felt even when she remained unseen. Monitors were mounted on the wall of the test kitchen, so we had a constant live feed of what was happening on set, which gave the kitchen a weird reverse Big Brother (or, in this case, Big Sister) feel. The monitors were in place for the show's benefit, so that we would be ready to deliver a particular portion or stage of a dish at exactly the appropriate time. When Martha pulled just-baked cookies out of her oven on the show, she actually *did* pull just-baked cookies out of her oven; the test kitchen made sure of it. And, if she demonstrated a Greek Easter bread that was made in endless stages, we in the kitchen had each and every one of those stages prepared at the appropriate times so that she would have the freedom to improvise and depart from the loose script. But the monitors meant that we could also see Martha respond to our unplanned inefficiencies or our poor choices. Nothing was worse than watching her bawl someone out for a mistake that, in hindsight, should not have happened. We eased our tension by occasionally poking fun at her on-screen performance, laughing at her hard "aitch" pronunciation on the word *herb,* getting the giggles any time she mentioned French beans after we pictured her French-kissing a string bean. I watched from the kitchen as she confused another fair-haired, petite freelancer for me, amazed that she could notice the smallest detail in the food or equipment but confuse two only vaguely similar people.

I learned a vast amount, and the experience with food styling and with live television production has proved to be invaluable. I loved the variety, too, of working with different foods each week as well as with so many different chefs, everyone from Madhur Jaffrey to Bobby Flay, who was as affable in real life as he appeared on television. I even had the opportunity to cook for President Clinton when he came to the compound to speak at a fund-raiser that Martha hosted for a local politician. We spent days preparing the perfect lunch, under the watchful eye of the many Secret Service members who surrounded the compound preparing for POTUS's arrival. It was impossible not to laugh at the absurdity of the situation: We were cooking for the President of the United States! We had presidential food tasters on the premises! It was one of the few times Martha actually joked around with us. It turned out that she, too, could do an imitation of the sunglasses-wearing Secret Service men who walked swiftly and purposefully, knees constantly bent, while simultaneously talking into their earpieces. Sadly for us, the show documenting our efforts for the presidential luncheon never aired because the Monica Lewinsky news broke just a few days before it was scheduled.

Despite all of the plusses of working with friends in the perfect kitchen for the best food show on television, I couldn't forget that I was in a corporate setting. Outside of the kitchen the mood was decidedly more proper, and office politics (always difficult for me) ruled. I never felt comfortable with the "outside" employees, who often turned to the kitchen to satisfy a chocolate craving, to have a cry, to simply find respite from the desk world. If I stayed on and tried to make a career in magazine or television test kitchens, I would have to learn to navigate those politics. I started to feel familiar pangs of envy whenever a restaurant chef came on as a guest. When Marcus Samuelsson came on the show, I wanted to tell him that I'd been a *real* cook and had even trailed for him years earlier. I wanted to tell Terrance Brennan that I had worked for his old chef de cuisine, Joey. Though I had left La Côte Basque after growing tired of restaurant life, after just six months away from it I felt myself longing for its excitement, purity, and, yes, prestige. Deep down, I didn't want to work for a TV show that hosted these chefs; I wanted to *be* a chef.

And then Joey called.

✦

THIRTEEN

Rising to the Occasion

H i, Doll, Joey's voice on my machine announced. *Gimme a buzz when you get this.* [Long pause.] *There's something I want to talk to you about.* Again with the cryptic messages.

Cursed with terminal punctuality, I arrived fifteen minutes early for my meeting with Joey at a bar in west Soho on that late summer afternoon. Fifteen minutes to prepare myself for the possibility that Joey was finally opening his own place and was going to offer me a job. Fifteen minutes to consider and reconsider the pros and cons of reentering the restaurant world. I ordered a pint of wheat beer, grabbed a small table outside, and waited.

When Joey finally sauntered up I was already halfway through my beer, thoughts fully convoluted. A tiny Yorkshire terrier lagged behind him at the end of a leash.

"Hi, Doll." He bent down to kiss my cheek. I suddenly realized that I had no idea how old Joey was. He could have been thirty, thirty-five. Maybe forty. Forty-five would be a stretch, a big one, but it was possible.

"This is Sassy," he said, picking up the small light brown dog, kissing it on the head. Sassy was his ex-girlfriend's.

"Jenny gave me visitation rights," he explained. He slipped Sassy's leash under a chair leg and set her under the small table while he got a beer. I gave Sassy my finger to sniff and she gave me a noncommittal dog kiss in return.

"You're drinking wheat, right, Doll?" Joey said, returning with a beer in each hand. I nodded, taking the glass. "I saw the lemon."

I gulped down what was left of my first beer, hoping the alcohol would calm my jumpy brain. I still wasn't sure if he had asked me there for a job. All of my mental straining might have been a complete waste of energy.

"So, Dolly," he said once seated and with Sassy on his lap. "How's Martha?"

"She's okay," I answered, suddenly worried that my every word carried an inordinate amount of weight. "There's good and bad, you know. I like the variety, meeting all the different chefs and stuff. But," I said, flipping the coin, "it's not, like, *really* cooking, you know? And the commute is sort of getting to me."

The two-hour commute hadn't been nearly as relaxing or conducive to reading as I'd anticipated. More often than not I was grumpy that I got home so late or that I had to get up at four a.m. to make the occasional seven a.m. start time. I was oversimplifying my ambivalence horrendously, but I wanted to leave every door open.

Being with Joey again reminded me of how much I'd enjoyed working for him. His quiet confidence, his aura of nonjudgment. Since my only real cooking job had been with him, he'd had an enormous impact on my confidence and capabilities. In my year at Layla, he'd not only encouraged me to progress and grow but had always found time for my questions and never condescended. When he joined us cooks for drinks after work, he left whatever friction had come up during service back in the kitchen and instead bought us rounds of beer and led the high fives. After working in a few restaurants, catering, and television, I realized that what I really, really wanted in a job—any job—was to be respected, guided, taught, and treated fairly. Joey had provided all of this.

"Well, Dolly, the reason I wanted to talk to you," he started, "is that I'm doing my own place."

Finally, he got down to it.

"I have the space and everything, Doll. It's on East Fifty-first Street, and it's going to be Mediterranean. You know, my kind of food."

Clearly excited, he went on to tell me all the details. He'd been introduced to his partner, Stan, a former maître d' of Restaurant Daniel, one of New York's very top restaurants, by a mutual friend. Joey would run the back of the house, and Stan, who had gathered all the financing and was the owner, would run the front. They'd found a space (and in New York City, opening a restaurant is all about the space, its location, and rent) that had been a restaurant before and were giving it a complete makeover, top to bottom, prep kitchen to dining room. They'd already been working on it for months and finally had a target opening date just six weeks away.

"So," he finally said. "I want you to be my pastry chef and help out with some cooking."

"I figure," he went on, "you learned enough pastry at Nobu, La Côte Basque, and the TV show to do the desserts. Plus, I have some ideas we can work on. I'll help you out."

Pastry chef? I'd assumed that he'd want me to cook. I kept listening.

"And, you already know my style of food and how I like to work, and that's really important. Frankie's coming on as sous-chef, so I'd want you to help him out, too." Frankie and I had overlapped at Layla for just a few weeks, but he had stayed on with Joey long after I left. I knew Frank was not only a good cook but a good guy all around.

"But mostly you'll be taking care of the desserts. Like I said, I have some ideas I want you to work on. Like . . ." he explained excitedly. "Like, I definitely want to have a rosewater crème brûlée, and we'll do the same almond milk ice that we had at Layla. Other than that, you're gonna come up with the rest of the menu. Your title," he finally said, "will be Pastry Chef." He paused.

Title? I got a title?

"It's gonna be a lot of work, Dolly. *A lot* of work. Openings always are. You'll be back in the Wild, Wild West of the restaurant world, but I think you, Frankie, and I will make a great team. Plus," he assured me, "you're a natural."

"What's it going to be called?" Oddly, it was the only question I could think of.

"Scarabée," he said regally and with purpose. I didn't understand the significance of the word.

"The name is my partner's idea," he explained, shrugging. "And he's set on it. It's the one thing he won't compromise on. I can live with it." He kept looking at me.

"So, Doll. I really want you to do it," he told me. "But I want you to think about it and call me in a few days."

Think about it. He said the same thing when he offered me the position of garde-manger and again when he suggested I move up to the grill position. *It's gonna be a challenge for you, Doll, working the grill. But think about it.* His challenges had always appealed to my ego. I'd taken the garde-manger job, and I'd worked the grill. But pastry chef? It was an entirely different ball game.

Despite my prejudice toward pastry early on in my career, I'd been drifting back into the dessert world ever since. Maybe it was kismet. Still, didn't most people work for many years toward the goal of earning the title of pastry chef? What about all the knowledge and techniques I needed to execute a full dessert menu? Had working at Nobu, La Côte Basque, and even MSLTV, where we did a fair amount of desserts, been enough?

I contemplated the prospect of returning to the Wild, Wild West of the restaurant world, as Joey called it. Was I ready to give up my three-day work week? Ready to deal with the pressure, once again, of performing at top speed every single day? The long hours?

The restaurant would be a big step for Joey, and it would surely receive press. What if I disappointed? "Downtown chef opens midtown spot . . . Hires unknown pastry chef who doesn't deliver . . . Jurgensen's desserts *suck*." But that was the worst-case scenario. What if I was actually good at it? I did have a lot of faith in the quality of my taste buds. I knew what tasted good, and that had to be worth something.

I realized that Joey wouldn't risk his own reputation if he didn't think I was up to the task. I started getting excited, and ideas kept popping into my head: chilled cherry-vanilla soup with mascarpone panna cotta, chocolate mousse with a white chocolate mousse center, warm pear tarte Tatin with *fromage blanc* ice cream. I'd always thought the tangy *fromage blanc* that Drew used in his cheesecake would make a great ice cream. I would have the chance to try it out for myself if I became Joey's pastry chef. Most exciting was the prospect of being responsible for my own menu, of really having an impact on a restaurant. I'd get to execute my own ideas, my own vision, all with Joey's lengthy and superlative experience as guidance, support, and safety net. Would there ever be a better scenario under which to take that sort of step?

Up to then, I'd gone back and forth between the two worlds, sweet and savory. I started out believing that I'd be better suited to working in the savory realm but eventually came to realize that my personality was ill-suited to becoming a chef, to being a leader in that sense. There was less power and prestige in the title of pastry chef, but there was also less pressure, and it was starting to feel like a perfect compromise. We hadn't talked about salary, health insurance, or any other particulars that were supposed to matter, but before I fell asleep that night, I knew my answer. I was going to be a pastry chef.

FOURTEEN

✦

Forbidden Fruit

Whack!

I slammed the narrow row of white plastic pyramid molds onto the edge of my stainless steel table—the full extent of Scarabée's basement pastry station—and crossed my fingers. I carefully lifted the molds to find that only three of the five chocolate mousse pyramids had come out of their molds.

I'd used the same kind of molds (production molds, they were called; each tray held seven rows of five and fit perfectly on a full sheet pan, making it easy to produce desserts in volume) at La Côte Basque, but there I'd used ovals that were bottomless and topless, which made them easy to unmold: I simply lined each oval with thin strips of plastic before filling the cavities with mousse, froze them, and then pushed each oval up and out. I had picked out the pyramid-shaped molds a few weeks earlier, thinking that a pyramid-shaped dessert would fit perfectly in a restaurant that was, after all, named for an Egyptian beetle. I immediately planned on filling each mold halfway with dark chocolate mousse, then piping in a secret center of white chocolate mouse, and finally filling in the bases of the pyramids with a thin, even layer of dark chocolate ganache made crunchy with crushed, roasted cocoa beans and crumbled halvah, a sesame candy. I had not, however, thought about how I would get the pyramids out of the molds. I started to worry: What kind of a pastry chef was I going to be if I couldn't even unmold my desserts?

I had tried brushing the insides of each cavity with melted cocoa butter, which made absolutely no difference. I'm not even sure how I came up with that stupid idea. I thought about lining each one with tempered chocolate, treating each pyramid like a giant individual bonbon, like the ones Jemal used to make. Not only would that take a lot of time (and chocolate), but it would work only if the chocolate was perfectly tempered and I didn't have enough faith in my tempering skills. Using a propane torch to heat the outsides of the pyramids was out of the question; the plastic would melt. I finally settled on running hot tap water over the pyramids just long enough to warm the mousse, then ran back to my table to—*whack!*—bang them out. Like most things I came up with at Scarabée, I figured out how to unmold the pyramids through trial and error. Over time, though, I was sure the trays would not be able to stand the beatings. But I would worry about that later. Only one week remained before opening day, and I was determined to prove myself, especially to the owner, a habitual

name dropper, who had suggested that his "friend" François Pay-
ard consult on the menu. I had to prove that I did not need any
outside help.

I had been working at Scarabée for weeks already before I
started to work on the desserts. Frank and I had been helping Joey
with the myriad preparations involved in opening a restaurant.
We functioned like cocaptains, and Joey included us in nearly
every decision he made, allowing us to see the process firsthand.
We met at nine every morning, bringing coffee back to the restaurant, still a construction site, where we spent most of the day. Joey
ordered the large equipment (ovens, refrigeration, mixers) and designed the layout of the kitchen and prep area. We had to anticipate what kind of small wares (small tools and equipment) we
would need, things I'd taken for granted in previous restaurants.
How many sheet pans would we need? Half sheet pans? Whisks?
Would we need four-ounce or two-ounce ladles or both? At
twenty dollars each, could I make do with just six silicone baking
mats? Yes, I probably could. We didn't want to forget anything:
rubber spatulas, fish spatulas, bains-marie, slotted spoons, sauce-
pans, sauté pans. Compiling one list was mind-boggling and
tedious.

Once the nitty-gritty of equipment was taken care of, we
moved on to more exciting things like menu ideas and talked
through every item, every garnish. We would have nine appetizers
and nine entrées, Joey said, but we needed to balance the heavy
dishes with the light, with foie gras at one end of the spectrum
and a plain green salad at the other. We hated the generic mesclun
salad—it was boring and unchallenging—but we knew that some

people always expected it to be available, so we put it on. Joey had the same philosophy with the entrées, so we begrudgingly included an entrée for those customers afraid of straying too far from the familiar. We referred to those unadventurous diners as "the chicken people."

Entrées decided, we wrestled with the menu wording: smashed vs. mashed, pan seared vs. pan roasted, housemade vs. homemade, crusted vs. coated. Written presentation was everything; if something didn't sound good, it wouldn't get ordered, no matter how delicious.

I labored over the desserts, wanting to create a varied menu that included something for everyone. Joey's idea for a rose petal crème brûlée meant there would be one custard. I wanted something frozen, a warm fruit dessert, and something light, like a fruit soup. I didn't want anything too generic or any overlap—if raspberries appeared on my chilled mango water with raspberry cream granita, then they would appear only on that dessert. And I had to have something chocolate; every dessert menu must have something chocolate, preferably something rich and decadent because that's what people want in a chocolate dessert. My desserts had to be simple; my skill level and experience demanded it. At that point, I simply had not yet amassed a giant tome of recipes to draw from like Glen and Jemal had, nor had I grown truly proficient at a lot of the more advanced techniques, like tempering chocolate. After working for only two pastry chefs, there was so much I did not yet know. But that didn't mean quality and taste had to suffer.

Once the kitchen was completed and in working order, we

peeled off the protective plastic coating that covered every stainless steel surface, cleaned off any dust, and unpacked the small wares. Finally, I started bringing my dessert ideas to fruition. I obsessed over every garnish, asking Joey and Frank to taste each version over and over. Was the cranberry compote I made to garnish the warm pear tarte Tatin sweet enough? Should I candy organic rose petals to go with the crème brûlée? Should I use more black olives in the focaccia? After a few attempts (my time at MSLTV proved to be invaluable for teaching me how to keep track of changes while developing a recipe), I came up with a great focaccia, one that turned out to be good enough to be served nightly.

It was hard work, and we spent every day, all day, working together. The restaurant became our existence and its success our only goal, while everything else in our respective lives took a backseat. It was exhausting and exhilarating; I actually felt that my contributions to the restaurant were important, that my ideas could impact its success. We worked so hard on every tiny detail in the hope that by the time diners finally sat down, their experience would be flawless, the food effortless.

"Doll," Joey said, surveying my tray of unmolded pyramids, "those look amazing! You were right about those molds."

"Thanks, Joey," I answered, not mentioning my trials with getting them out. I wanted him to think I knew what I was doing.

"We got less than a week left, Doll. Why don't we clean up and get out of here, enjoy what's left of the night? Frank's already on his way out," he offered.

I didn't argue. I knew that once we opened, our free time would be reduced to nil. I cleaned up, and we left the restaurant together.

"Hey, Doll," said Joey as we headed to the downtown subway. "You wanna see a movie tonight?"

We'd been spending so much time together that I was no longer intimidated or afraid of my boss. Maybe we actually could become friends, or work friends at the very least. A movie sounded great.

I met him at a small independent theater downtown, and afterward we walked for a few blocks, enjoying the warm summer evening. When I felt his hand on my back a few times, I chalked it up to subtle chivalry; he had four older sisters, after all. I thought nothing of it when he invited me up to his apartment for a Heineken and we sat on his couch and let out some of the frustration that had been building up over the previous weeks. We complained about some of the owner's decisions. We thought he spent far too much money on an interior designer, money that might have been better saved as working capital to get us through slow times, if they came. I complained about his insistence on listing every menu item in French first, with a translation below. He thought it lent an upscale feel. I found it not only pretentious but also tedious. Who wanted to sift through all that French to find out if they wanted striped bass or snapper? And he wore acid-wash jeans and cowboy boots. Who was he kidding?

Somehow, amid the laughter and the exhaustion, Joey's strong hands were rubbing my shoulders. Somehow, we were kissing. Somehow my shirt came off, and he carried me into his bed. I woke up the next morning at daybreak and sneaked out before he woke up so I could shower and change clothes at home before heading in to work.

I never thought anything like that would happen. He was my *chef.* My boss! Sure, I thought he was handsome, but I didn't want to *date* him. Did I? Then again, I hadn't stopped him that night, either, and I'd had a million reasons to do so. I put it out of my mind and figured we had an unspoken agreement to simply pretend it never happened.

"I hope you're okay about the other night, Doll," Joey said two days later as we were leaving work. *Doll.* Somehow my nickname took on a new subtlety since we'd slept together. I looked up at him.

"Yeah, sure," I answered, with all the nonchalance I could muster. "I'm okay."

"Good," he said, "because I really like working with you, Doll. I'd hate to mess that up." I took that to be definitive: It was just something that happened, a tiny bump in the road of our professional relationship and our potential friendship.

"Sure," I agreed.

"I mean," he went on, "I've always found you really attractive."

Maybe it was more than a bump? Why did he have to add *that*? I tried to ignore it.

"Thanks," was all I could muster.

That was the end of the conversation. We returned to business as usual. We talked about food, made decisions, worked on menus, prepared for the opening and the crucial first weeks. I let it go, determined not to let it interfere with my work.

✦

FIFTEEN

Seeing Stars

She sidled into the kitchen, casually making her way over to the expediter station, where Joey stood taking command of the kitchen. It was Camille, the twenty-year-old French coat-check girl at Scarabée, in her usual "uniform": snug, low-cut shirt and even snugger black pants. She walked right up to Joey, practically wrapping her lithe body around him. She coyly posed whatever question she'd come up with as an excuse to leave her coat-check post and come back to the kitchen, where the real work happens. Joey's eyes remained fixed on the dupe slide, which held the order tickets for every table seated in the dining room. As expediter, he was at the helm of the kitchen, funneling ordering information to the cooks, but he was also a liaison between the waiters and kitchen and all special requests or questions had to go through him and only him. The cooks had to remain focused on their pickups, and the waiters had to wait for his direction before taking food out of the kitchen. If there is a linchpin in a busy kitchen, it is the expediter. Joey listened to Camille while he continued to manage the dupes: crossing out appetizers as they left the kitchen, noting times, "spiking" tickets when a table's order had been completed.

Camille stood close to him—too close. Her eyes fluttered up at him as she waited. Eyes still on the dupes, Joey cracked a slight, wry smile, and I watched him mouth the word *okay,* which transformed Camille's expectant face into a wide grin. She turned and pranced out of the kitchen, her full, perfect ass the last of her to go. I realized with a sudden pang of nausea that Camille and Joey had slept together. Worse: They'd *been* sleeping together.

"Fuckin' hot!" said Vinnie in a loud stage whisper.

We'd been open only six weeks and already the line cooks were comfortable in their new setting, each one taking on a role. Vinnie, the heavily accented Brooklyn native, was the only cook adept enough at his job to not only notice and comment on every female who entered the kitchen but also simultaneously put up twelve perfectly executed entrées. He had a smart, streetwise answer for everything and everyone, aside from Joey, for whom he had great respect. The rest of the cooks idolized him. I didn't need any verbal confirmation of Camille's hotness, but I was helpless. I could no sooner shut up Vinnie than I could ignore him.

"Is that ready?" Marlene's voice snapped me back to reality. "The dessert," she went on. "Can I take it? My table's in a rush. Pre-theater," she explained.

I looked down at the warm pear tart Tatin oozing caramel, my right hand poised above the plate, a scoop of *fromage blanc* ice cream ready to finish the dessert. I hated to put the ice cream on warm desserts before I had someone ready to pick them up.

I squeezed my right palm around the scoop and, with a flip of my wrist, let the ice cream fall onto the warm Tatin. With my left hand, I wedged a chunk of pecan brittle into the ice cream. Done.

"Ready," I told Marlene. She quickly headed back to the dining room.

I looked over at Joey. He was so talented, standing there keeping watch over his kitchen. He was calm and commanding and fair, stern but sometimes playful. The cooks respected him, the waiters adored him, and all the women vied for his attention. We had been open for six weeks, and everyone wanted to be his favorite. Even women working in neighborhood offices had shown up for lunch waving his photo from a recent local magazine review. He charmed them all, including me.

Aside from the brief conversation a few days after "that night," Joey and I never talked about what had happened between us, we simply went back to work. Judging from the amount of press we'd already gotten, our public relations company was doing its job. Scarabée had been featured in plenty of local magazines, and Joey's photo had been featured almost as often as his food. The restaurant had been relatively busy since opening night, and as a result I'd been too busy maintaining my dessert station and helping out with the kitchen to worry about what had happened between Joey and me. Until Camille walked in that night.

At my spot at the dessert station, I was perfectly poised to watch the younger, clean-smelling Camille cozy up to Joey. I was ten hours into yet another fourteen-hour day, in my uniform of super baggy chef's pants reminiscent of MC Hammer and shapeless chef's coat (the smallest size available is still too big for me), my short hair pomaded into place, and my forearms sticky with sugar and covered in burns. Camille's freshly shampooed, flowing hair was framing her face and big doe eyes. I felt about as far from fucking hot as possible, and I couldn't believe I was jealous. What had I been thinking, sleeping with my chef? Was I stupid? I knew that sooner or later he'd find someone else to be with and that, given the close quarters and long hours in which we worked, I'd find out about it. I hadn't counted on actually having to watch.

I pushed the uncomfortable reality out of my head and went back to work. I pulled a bowl of pistachio biscotti dough out of the refrigerator beneath me and plopped it onto the stainless steel counter. If I could finish rolling out the dough into logs at night during my down time, it would be ready to bake the next morning. I'd be one step ahead of the game, and keeping up with the heavy workload was all about staying one step ahead, using every available second. Using a curved, plastic bowl scraper, I cut off a hunk of the stiff dough, dusted the table with a sprinkle of flour, and dropped the dough onto the floured surface.

But rolling out logs of biscotti dough did little to distract me from the harsh reality that Camille had brought with her when she'd sashayed into the kitchen. I suddenly saw myself as just one of many employees Joey had taken home. I was a cliché. Worse, I shared the honor with the ultimate restaurant cliché: the coat-check girl, the easiest hookup in the business. And she was French, too. Before I knew it, I was replaying my night with Joey in my head, trying to remember all the details, looking for clues in the hope that it actually meant something to him.

I gently caressed the ball of dough outward while keeping the pressure even with each hand. I remembered his thick fingers in my hair, my mouth on his neck. I slowly worked each stump, stretching the dough outward into long, thick, even logs. I lined them up evenly on a half sheet pan lined with parchment paper. I pictured my hands on his . . .

"Doll!" commanded Joey. I looked up from the biscotti. "Give Rob a hand."

Rob (aka Rob the Slob) had been working garde-manger for more than two weeks and hadn't yet learned how to work efficiently or neatly. Since our stations were right next to each other, he became my responsibility. I quickly rinsed off my hands and wiped my table free of flour and residual dough. Then I glanced at the tickets hanging in Rob's station and looked down at the plates he'd begun in front of him.

"What about the cherries?" I asked. Caught like a deer in headlights, he stopped his shuffling and looked up at me. He was a mess. He moved way more than he needed to, using three motions when one efficient move would have sufficed. He was the kind of cook who always had a filthy apron and always seemed out of breath. He hated having to answer to a girl.

"The dried cherries," I specified, "for the duck confit salad?"

He stood still for a moment, looking painfully at the duck salad, wanting so badly for me to be wrong. I was not.

"Fix it," I told him.

He turned away with his head down, plucked a few of the bright red cherries from his *mise-en-place,* and added them to the salad, then pushed the plate forward so it could be picked up by the food runner, Sayid. I assessed the dupes hanging in front of him and put up two green salads (I was still amazed at how many of the ordinary salads we sold), a salmon tartare, and a warm goat cheese and golden beet salad. He was in the weeds already, and it wasn't even crunch time. I washed the vinaigrette off my hands and took my tray of biscotti logs downstairs.

By the time I returned, the printer was beginning its steady staccato, informing us that the dining room was filling up. Joey's voice took on that "don't fuck around" tone as he called out appetizer orders.

"Rob!" he demanded. "Pick up two green—one SOS; three duck; three tartare; and a beet—no onions on that beet."

He reached into Rob's station and added copies of the new tickets to the dupe slide, framing his station with a curtain of white paper rectangles across the top. I stepped in, before Rob drowned in a swirl of mesclun greens, chianti vinaigrette, and chopped herbs. Not wanting to be reprimanded in front of everyone again, he silently stepped aside and let me help.

While we worked on the appetizers, Joey continued calling out orders, forewarning the rest of the cooks of their upcoming pickups.

"Vinnie!" he boomed. "On order: two salmon—one medium, one mid-rare; a squabie; and three filet, two mid-rare and one well done."

"Well done?" Vinnie snapped without losing a single second of precious time and without a slip of his smile. "Who the fuck eats filet well done?"

"Some asshole from Jersey," answered Billy from the hot appetizer station. "It *is* Saturday night!"

"Frank," Joey continued, ignoring their banter and directing the orders at Frank, who worked the sauté station in the middle of the line. "You got two pasta, four—that's four—bass. Jeez, they love that bass. And two cod. And while you're at it, fire tables thirty-two and fourteen. Let's get their food outta here before the next big pickup."

I helped Rob get his appetizers out while keeping one eye on every plate he put together. Before long, the kitchen became a swirl of controlled chaos—chaotic to an untrained eye, and controlled by Joey. Everyone, aside from poor Rob, was working with practiced movement, careful not to waste a single turn.

"How many miles do you think we walk each night here, just within our own little station?" joked Vinnie.

"Five miles," piped up Billy. Vinnie looked at him incredulously.

Billy shrugged. "I wore a pedometer once. Just to see."

Vinnie was about to razz him: What kind of a loser wears a pedometer to work? The cooks seemed to thrive on a constant flow of teasing, dissing, and practical jokes, though Vinnie had yet to be the butt of any of these. He was the one who poured Tabasco (or salt or white vinegar) into Billy's iced coffee when he wasn't looking, and it was Vinnie who humiliated any waiter who dared to complain, giving voice to the collective exasperation of the cooks who worked twice as long and earned half as much money. His mocking voice sent waiters running out of the kitchen.

"Keep it down, guys," Joey interceded. "Pay attention to the food."

More tickets. More calls. Plates clinked, pans clanked, but otherwise the kitchen became quiet with intent. No more banter.

Suddenly the owner was in the kitchen standing next to Joey, exactly where Camille had been not too long before, talking into his ear. He turned and left the kitchen. Joey looked down for a moment, then headed toward my station. I left Rob alone to meet him. He looked serious.

"Doll," he said, standing close, "I want you to go downstairs and get two of every dessert on your menu, garnishes, too, the best you've got. They have to be perfect."

He paused, leaning in. "*She's* here."

"She" was Ruth Reichl, the restaurant critic for the *New York Times,* the most prestigious reviewer we could get. I couldn't believe the moment had actually arrived.

"Yes," was all I could say.

Then he said, "Come back upstairs. I'm gonna need your help up here."

I ran downstairs, thinking of nothing else besides collecting my desserts and making a good impression. It is the day that every ambitious restaurant hopes for. Both Joey and the owner knew what she looked like, and for those who didn't, they'd posted an old photocopy of her face that had been passed through the restaurant world. We also had a list of known aliases she'd used in the past, as well as some phone and credit card numbers that had gone with them. Though we all like to believe that every single diner receives equal treatment and food, the reality is that no one gets the complete and utter devotion and focus of the entire restaurant staff like the critic from the *New York Times*.

I was back upstairs in five minutes, desserts in hand, searching through my candied rose petals for the most beautiful specimens, picking over my various tuiles for those that were perfectly baked and formed. I planned every inch of each plate.

"Okay," said Joey, pulling the dupe out of the printer. "This is her table: twenty-three. VIP! Pick up! One goat, one duck, one tartare, and a crab crêpe. Got it?" He looked over at me. I nodded. Regardless of what had happened between us personally, we still had full communication in the kitchen: I knew exactly what to do and how to do it.

Rob had already pulled down the appropriate plates when I stepped over to his station. He looked up at me. Joey looked at him. Rob looked at Joey.

"Let Doll take care of this table, okay, Rob?" he said sternly and unapologetically. Rob stepped aside, head hung down.

I carefully composed the salads, making sure that each leafy green was perfect, each tender morsel of duck confit free of gristle, the Gorgonzola perfectly crumbled and evenly distributed. I tasted everything (tasting is the only way to really know if there's enough salt; in fact, diners should hope that the cooks' fingers have been in everything they're eating), adjusted the seasoning, styled the plates. I aimed for that ideal salad pile that simultaneously looks architectural and completely effortless.

The goat cheese plate was all about color. After Billy handed me the small puck of warm pan-seared goat cheese, I mixed a salad of roasted golden and red beets, frisée, chives, and pickled red onions and gently molded it into a ball on top of the goat cheese, almost like a tiny tumbleweed. I dotted the naked border of the plate alternately with an intensely purple beet reduction, vibrant green chive oil, and syrupy black balsamic reduction. Spiced candied walnuts were the final touch. The salmon tartare was the quickest. The chopped raw salmon, avocado purée, caviar, and crème fraîche had been layered in a two-inch-high cylinder before service started. I simply unmolded it onto a circle of thinly sliced and flash-marinated cucumbers. With a final wipe of each plate's edges, I pushed the appetizers forward, where Joey had been watching, waiting. He nodded his approval, then called to the most reliable food runner to deliver the first course to table twenty-three.

"Sayid," Joey told him sternly. "This is a very important table, understand?"

"Yes, Chef," he answered. Though still young, Sayid was a veteran food runner and took his job very seriously. He kept his plates perfectly balanced and paid meticulous attention to detail. "I know," he assured.

"I want *you* to clear the table," Joey instructed him. "And I want to see their finished plates before you drop them off at the dish station."

"Yes, Chef."

"Okay, Sayid. Go.

"Okay, guys," Joey continued. "Whatever you got working

right now, get it out. I want everyone to be able to focus on twenty-three. It's gotta be perfect."

By the time twenty-three was ready for its entrées, the cooks had their pans hot on the stove, their proteins pulled out of the refrigerators and seasoned, their most perfect garnishes chosen. When the call to fire the table came, everything else was put aside, and the four entrées for twenty-three became the only thing that mattered. Joey left his post and stepped behind the line to oversee every detail.

"Doll!" he directed, nodding his head toward the expediting station.

I took my cue and filled in for him while he helped out with the entrées. I kept track of new tickets coming in, fielded any questions from the waiters, kept an eye on Rob, who had been left to tackle incoming appetizers on his own, and got the last-minute touches ready for twenty-three's entrées: a tiny quenelle of thickened yogurt, a perfect sprig of chervil, a dollop of caviar.

Camille was probably standing vacantly in her coat-check area, smiling hopefully at the customers as they came and went, laughing at whatever they might say. She probably didn't even read the *New York Times,* let alone know who was *at* table twenty-three. Maybe she was fucking hot, but her job was to stand around and smile, take a coat, match a number now and then. She'd even been banned from answering the phones ever since we found out she'd giggled in response to a customer wanting to change a reservation: *I am sooo sorreeee! I do not speak English vereee well!* She'd never be trusted to oversee the dupes or be relied on to make food for the *New York Times* critic. Maybe I wasn't fucking hot, even without my shapeless chef's coat, but at least I made a contribution. No one would put her name in a review.

After twenty-three's entrée plates came back much like the appetizers—mostly clean, aside from an only partially emptied marrow bone, over which Joey obsessed—I got the dessert order: tarte Tatin, crème brûlée, pyramid, pomegranate bombe. I slid a tart Tatin into the oven and with a practiced and steady hand, I plated each dessert under Joey's watchful eye.

I shook an even layer of white sugar onto the surface of the crème brûlée and burned it to an even, deep brown with a propane torch. Quickly, before the caramel set up, I placed two perfect candied rose petals on the crust. It was such a simple dessert, but I didn't want it to seem as though I had overlooked its plate, so I carefully stacked four small pieces of pistachio biscotti in the shape of a crisscross next to it.

On to the pyramid. I carefully set the chocolate mousse pyramid in the center of a round white plate. I'd sprayed the pyramids with milk chocolate, which gave them a sandy-looking coating, appropriate for a pyramid, I thought. The garnishes were simple: a large dot of blackberry sauce in the front of the plate and a round vanilla tuile that had streaks of purple running across stuck into the pyramid. The tuile appeared to be a setting sun and the blackberry sauce its reflection on the plate. The final touch was a small triangle of halvah.

The pomegranate bombe, a dome of frozen lemon verbena parfait with a ball of pomegranate sorbet hiding in its center, was my favorite plate of all. I set the dome on top of a smaller almond *dacquoise* (a crunchy meringue) so that it appeared to be hovering just an inch above the plate. Then I stuck sliced almonds into the bottom edge of the dome, so they splayed out in a circular pattern. The result, floating over the plate with a river of pomegranate reduction and crème anglaise below, looked like something out of *The Jetsons.*

By the time the three were done, my tart Tatin was warm. I turned it upside down and onto its plate, quickly made a perfect quenelle of *fromage blanc* ice cream, which I set on the Tatin, and gave the nod to Sayid. My desserts were ready to meet their fate, as was I. Everything I'd worked for thus far culminated in that moment when the critic feasted her eyes on what I hoped she would think were great-looking and even better-tasting desserts. Taste was my number one priority, but I cared about how they looked, too, knowing that a customer could be sold on a dessert just by seeing it pass by in the dining room. I'd tried to make all of my desserts slightly playful and not too fussy. I was proud.

"Good job, everyone," said Joey. "Now let's finish up the night."

Once the last customer was fed and table twenty-three's dessert plates returned (mostly cleaned, aside from a half-eaten pyramid, over which I then obsessed), we peeled off our night's worth of sweat and returned to the clothes of regular people. We all—waiters and cooks alike—needed a drink and headed out to the corner bar for some unwinding. We replayed the night over and over. Who spotted her first? The owner. Good call! What alias did she use? Marge Hooper. It got added to our list and passed on to our friends in other restaurants. Was she nice? Polite. Did she know we were on to her? Nobody knew.

After an hour, I was spent. Tired from the long workday, the overwhelming conversation that surrounded me in the bar, the excitement, and the booze. And from my earlier bird's-eye view of Camille acting so cozy with Joey. She wasn't such a bad person, I knew that deep down. I guess I just hadn't really let go of my own night with Joey.

I grabbed my bag and sneaked out, avoiding the hassle of a long group good-bye. I decided to treat myself and take a cab home to Brooklyn, cutting my travel time by two thirds. My head, still stuffy with thoughts of the restaurant, welcomed the fresh, early October air. I stood at the curb with one arm raised over my head and waited for an available cab. Cabs were harder to come by at the late hour but I didn't mind waiting a few minutes.

"Doll!" Joey's voice came from the bar's doorway. I turned and saw him standing alone, half inside the bar, half out. He walked toward me.

"Sneaking out?" he asked.

"Yeah," I told him. "Too many people, you know?"

"Yeah," he said. "I know."

A cab finally pulled up, and I opened the door.

"Doll," he said again. I waited, hand on the door.

"I couldn't have done it without you," he said. "You know that, right, Doll?"

Did I? I wanted to. "Okay," is all I said.

"Have a good night, Doll," he said. "Get home safe." He kissed me with a quick squeeze before heading back inside.

I got into the waiting cab, the driver looking bored.

"I'm going to Williamsburg," I told him. "Second exit after the bridge." He took off down Second Avenue.

I sank into the backseat of the cab, tired and ready to be alone in my apartment, looking forward to getting some sleep before having to get up and do it all again. The critic would have to come back before she'd have enough information for the review, and I needed to be ready.

✦

SIXTEEN

Check, Please

The *Times* critic made three more visits (any critic worth her salt makes multiple visits in order to sample a wide range of food and to test the consistency), and she was spotted every time. When the paper called to schedule a photo of the dining room during dinner service, we knew for sure that the review would appear the following Wednesday, so we had six days to agonize with anticipation. What was done was done; our fate rested in her hands. The most we could do was make sure that the dining room looked busy on the night of the photo, so we all asked friends to come in for dinner at the appointed time. The last thing we wanted was a photo of an empty room—how would that look?

Late on the night before the review was to appear, Joey left work to buy the paper from a twenty-four-hour newsstand. He'd scoped out which newsstand was the first to receive the earliest edition of the paper. He wanted to be the first to read the review, and he wanted to do it in solitude, just in case. The rest of us waited in the kitchen, glasses of wine and beer in hand, ready to celebrate— or drown our sorrows. What if she'd hated my desserts? Not only would I have failed, but it would be a public failure, in writing, for the entire world to see. I had a second glass of wine.

But Joey returned triumphant, and with an enormous, satisfied smile he held up the paper to us with a sigh of relief.

"Two stars!"

Two stars from the *New York Times* was a definite triumph. After a collective cheer we gathered around him as he read the entire review out loud, savoring each word of praise for his delicious food. She swooned over the lamb sandwich (one of my favorites, too), a flat disc of grilled dough stuffed with cinnamon-braised lamb, hummus, *tadzhiki*, greens, preserved lemon, and cucumbers, calling it "the best sandwich I ever tasted." She praised his fricassee of rabbit with green lentils and the pomegranate-glazed salmon. She applauded the grilled baby octopus salad with fingerling potatoes and pickled onions, an appetizer that was a kitchen favorite, too, not least of all because the tiny octopus bodies that we discarded (only the bouquets of eight tiny legs were used) made perfect finger puppets. She even loved my focaccia.

I waited anxiously. Desserts always came last.

The owner was happy that he'd been praised for his fine selection of boutique wines and the service, and that she'd acknowledged his restaurant pedigree. Her only criticism so far was the phrasing of the menu: She found it too wordy and cumbersome, especially the dual French-English dinner menu. I wanted to yell out "I told you so," but I didn't. It was a minor criticism and a matter that could be easily remedied.

It was all wonderful, but I couldn't breathe until I heard about the desserts. Joey kept reading: *Desserts are classics that have been re-imagined with Middle Eastern flavors and are gorgeously arranged.*

"She loved them, Doll," praised Joey, putting his arm around me.

I stood there and smiled. It was a simple comment on my work, not gushing or superlative, perhaps, like I might have hoped it would be, but it was good. According to the review, my goal in creating Scarabée's desserts had been achieved. I was the tiniest bit disappointed that my name had not appeared, but could I really complain? My desserts were "gorgeous," and she hadn't said a single negative thing about them.

As we hoped, the stellar review brought in business almost immediately, and we happily adjusted to the increase. In the following months, we were reviewed multiple times, and reading each one for the first time was exhilarating. I savored every moment of it. My name did eventually appear, and my ego swelled with pride every time my work was recognized for being "delicious," "divine," "fabulous." I shamelessly told my friends about every review, demanding that they buy the magazines and newspapers to see for themselves.

I faxed the reviews from major publications to my mother in Tennessee, so she, too, could read for herself of my success. Every positive review served as validation: Trading in office life and becoming a pastry chef had been the right choice. My parents didn't have to worry; I had succeeded in my new career. It was right there in black and white.

With so much positive feedback appearing in print, it should have been easy to brush off the occasional slur, but ego is a fragile thing. For us, cooking was all about achieving perfection: the perfect taste, the perfect plate, the perfect meal, and having someone, especially the less respected writers who had probably never themselves worked in a restaurant, disparage any part of it was hard to swallow.

Despite the glut of good reviews, the few bad comments stuck in my side like thick, stubborn thorns. I was outraged when a writer from a local free paper trashed my pear tarte Tatin. This same writer had made multiple errors in the food descriptions, mistaking currants for raisins, for example. How dare such a lazy writer be able to judge my work? I bellyached about it for days, despite Joey's urging that I let it go: *Nobody who matters cares about that restaurant column, Doll. It's in a free paper! People don't even pay for it!* But I couldn't let it go until finally, arriving home after work one night, I found my answering machine blinking with a single message. Joey had left a loop recording of a snippet from Ruth Reichl's radio show in which she gave a brief review of the restaurant: *the pear tart was quite delicious . . . the pear tart was quite delicious . . . the pear tart was quite delicious.*

Reviews led to interview requests. "Doll," urged Joey after we'd been interviewed together, "you gotta stop telling people that you don't like sweets. It doesn't sound good."

During an interview with a local radio host I'd been asked what my favorite dessert to eat was. I was honest. I didn't really eat many sweets; they no longer tempted me. Aside from an occasional bit of ice cream or a cookie, I'd much rather have a steak or fries or even sautéed spinach with garlic.

"You're like a drug dealer who doesn't do drugs," he added.

"But it's true," I told him. "And it doesn't mean that I don't like making them or that I don't know what tastes good."

"Doll, you have one of the best senses of quality I've ever seen. But just think about it. How it sounds, you not liking desserts. Sometimes you just have to pretend a little."

It wasn't the only time Joey encouraged me to "pretend a little." If a writer called about an article she was writing on a particular ingredient, figs, for example, and asked if I used them on my menu, I was instructed to answer an emphatic "yes" and spontaneously invent a dessert that included that ingredient that I could then talk about. I could always put it on the menu after the fact, Joey said. That way I'd get included in the article and get the exposure. The more exposure, the better.

As a result of all the good press, we enjoyed an increase in business and therefore, a decrease in stress levels. My routines were set, I was comfortable with my desserts, and I even hired someone to work at night plating them. Finally I had my nights free, and my life resembled something almost normal. I pretended that I had never slept with Joey and had never been jealous of the Frenchie. Eventually, I started dating other people—outside of the business.

Joey and I still saw each other every day and worked together closely. Over time, we became an ideal team, able to work together on any task, our strengths complimenting each other's perfectly. I fully accepted his authority, and he in turn always treated me with respect. I looked up to him, eager to learn anything I could from his fifteen years of experience, and he valued my computer and writing skills, my patience, my taste buds. Gradually, we developed a deeper friendship, too, and began talking on the phone. By the time summer rolled around, we were spending our mutual day off together, usually at the beach with a group of our friends, some of them in the restaurant business, others not. We became super-friends, friends on steroids. Even our friends became suspicious that there was something more.

I suppose it was only a matter of time before we once again crossed that line, and I should have seen it coming. I *did* see it coming, but I looked the other way. That night, after a long day at the beach, I didn't have to go back to Joey's under the pretense of wanting to take a shower before going out to have a bite to eat (as if spending the entire day together hadn't been enough). I *could* have gotten dressed in his bathroom instead of coming out of the shower in just my towel to get my change of clothes. And I *could* have turned away from Joey when I saw that look in his heavy hazel eyes, the look I *should* have remembered from almost a year earlier. But I didn't.

After that night, sleepovers became common, simply an extension of the time we already spent together, but nothing else changed. We remained a perfect team at work and never talked about what was going on between us. It just kept happening, unaffected at first by the gradual slowing of business. But when business began to slow, so did our morale. We tried in vain to figure out the problem. Was it the name? I'd been worried about naming the restaurant after a bug, even if it was a French-sounding one, and my fears were realized every time a delivery man announced he had a package for "Scrabby's." Maybe it was the location, though it was unlikely. There was nothing wrong with the food or service, we were sure of that, thanks to consistent affirmation in the press. Maybe New York City was simply too fickle a restaurant town, and our customers had moved on to the next new place. The early success we'd experienced had slipped through our fingers and been washed away, and we all felt the blow, especially the owner.

Eventually, things between Joey and the owner became irrevocably strained until finally Joey accepted an offer to open a new restaurant in a hotel just a few blocks away. Frank and I, utterly loyal to our chef, gave notice, too. We'd come in as a team and we left the same way.

SEVENTEEN

✦

Table for Two

Not long before I started working at the hotel, Joey and I were having dinner at a "friends-and-family" night, one of my favorite industry perks. In exchange for constructive criticism and professional feedback on everything from food to service to lighting, a soon-to-be-open restaurant provides colleagues with a complimentary dinner. It is a system that gives new restaurants a brief chance to work out their kinks before real customers and, even more important, the critics show up.

Since the demise of Scarabée, our amorphous relationship, which consisted of sleepovers, social outings, and work-related conversation, had only grown stronger, despite the fact that each of us silently resolved not to talk about what was going on. It wasn't until Sal, the restaurant's manager and a friend of Joey, introduced us to some fellow diners that I was suddenly forced to acknowledge the reality of the situation.

"This is Joey," Sal said to the two couples seated at the table next to us. "He was the chef at Layla and Scarabée. And this," he continued, "is his girlfriend, Dalia."

Girlfriend? I noticed Joey stiffen at the sudden designation hanging in the air, and I felt a little bit panicky at the prospect of being outed. That single word, which up to now had remained unspoken, abruptly gave name to a situation I'd pretended didn't exist and one that, judging by his reaction to the label, Joey wasn't keen on acknowledging either. We both nodded at the table, *Nice to meet you.* Why had Sal said that? Of course Joey and I had bumped into friends and industry people during the many hours we spent together, but we'd always observed an unspoken rule to limit any affection beyond what was appropriate to our relationship as friendly coworkers. I was always introduced as Joey's pastry chef (it was not unusual for a chef to work with the same pastry chef from job to job, since it could be difficult to find a good match). The last thing I wanted was for anyone to think that I'd been hired as Joey's pastry chef just because we were dating. Pastry chef was a title I'd worked hard for and one that I valued— and one that got a lot more respect than "girlfriend."

We left the restaurant in silence. Neither one of us said anything, in fact, until I was at the corner hailing a cab. Normally after a dinner out, we'd get into the same cab and go back to the same apartment, where we would discard all the unspoken pretenses and get into the same bed. When the cab pulled up, though, I was so frustrated with myself for being in this situation and with him for letting me (he was the chef, the one in a position of authority, wasn't it his responsibility to respect boundaries?) that I practically ran to the cab that pulled up a few feet in front of me.

"Wait, Doll," I heard Joey say as I walked toward the cab. "Where are you going?" He was smiling, as if nothing had happened. Typical.

"Home," I answered, turning back to my cab. "I'm going home." I slammed the door.

It took twenty minutes to get home to Brooklyn, twenty minutes in which I thought about what an idiot I'd been. I'd been loath to think too deeply about our relationship, for fear I'd be forced to acknowledge the very real possibility that the addendum to our perfect work friendship meant nothing more to Joey than a simple convenience or, worse, that I might be just one of many women he was "friends" with.

The truth was that I'd been enjoying all of our time together and I didn't want to risk ruining it by splitting hairs over its definition. There was so much more than work that held us together. We saw things the same way, appreciated the little things and the bigger ones, too. He had been generous in every sense of the word, helping me fix things around my apartment, driving me for errands, taking me out for countless dinners and movies, always resisting my pleas to pay for something. *Save your money, Doll,* he always said. *Buy yourself something nice.* He took care of me. He was adorable and manly and talented and ambitious and perfect, and I had done the unthinkably stupid: I had fallen for my chef.

Idiot.

To make matters worse, in just a few days I would officially start my new job as pastry chef at the hotel with Joey. Another restaurant opening, which meant another extended, stressful period of long hours working closely together. Not exactly the ideal situation in which to work out personal feelings for a boss, especially when those feelings might not be reciprocated.

By the time I got home at nearly midnight, there was already a message from Joey on my machine. *Gimme a buzz when you get in, Doll. I gotta ask you something.* It was the same message I'd gotten nearly every night for the past few months. How did he manage to sound so vague and yet so endearing? Of course, I called. He picked up on the first ring.

"Hi, Doll," he said. "What's going on?" He sounded almost cheerful.

"What do you mean?" I answered. He *had* to know what's going on, didn't he? I hated him for pretending that he hadn't cringed at hearing me called his girlfriend.

"You seemed so angry, Doll. When you left." He sounded superficially concerned. He was probably worried that I would quit, that he'd have to find a new pastry chef in a few days. He was going to make me bring it up. I braced myself.

"What are we doing?" I finally said.

"What do you mean, Doll?" he said. "You're my best friend." Great. I was his best friend. I'd heard it a million times before. *You're my best friend.* This was going nowhere.

"Yeah, Joey, I know," I said purposefully. "But what are we *doing?*"

Nothing. He *had* to know what I was getting at, but he made me spell it out.

"Joey," I started again. "We spend every day together. We talk on the phone *every* night." I paused. "We have sleepovers."

More silence.

"What are we doing?" I said louder, gaining momentum. "You seemed horrified when Sal introduced me as your girlfriend, and I know we never talk about it, but if what we're doing isn't dating or whatever, then aren't we wasting our time? How can either one of us meet someone to be with for real if we spend every single minute together? Talk every night on the phone? I just can't keep doing this if it doesn't mean anything."

Still more silence. I was getting worked up, aware that I was on the verge of sounding like a crazy drunk girl and I did not want to be *that* girl. I took a breath.

"I'm just saying, Joey, that we have to decide." Okay. I was going to do it. I was only going to say it once. "Either we do it for real, or we stop now and we go back to being friends. *Just* friends."

"It's complicated, Doll," he said.

"I need to know what's going on with us, Joey. My head is full," I explained. "In a few days I start working with you at the hotel, and I need to know where I stand before then."

Joey was quiet on the other end of the line. I could practically see him pacing, rubbing his thumb back and forth across the other fingers on that hand, the way he did when he tried to figure something out, turning his head from side to side, considering all the options.

"Can't you just come over, Doll?" he finally said. "Just get in a car and come over."

"Did you hear anything I just said?" I said impatiently.

"Yeah, Doll," he said, more calmly. "I want you to come over."

I tried to decipher what he meant until he clarified.

"I don't want to meet anybody else." Finally, I was the quiet one.

"Does that mean you want to do this? That you want me to be your *girlfriend?*" Saying the word out loud felt dangerous, but I needed to be sure. Absolutely sure. There was a pause. A long pause. Long as death.

"Yes, Doll. Please just get in a car and come over right away."

I hung up the phone, dialed a car service, and grabbed some clean underwear.

✦

EIGHTEEN

Reservations

With a flick of my wrist I flipped the banana tart Tatin over and waited for the caramel-laden banana slabs to fall elegantly onto the fat pillow of puff pastry that sat waiting for them on the plate below. Nothing. My previous attempt resulted in a caramel that was far too runny, and as a result I had overcompensated and made the caramel too hard. I tossed the useless Tatin into a bucket of water to soak and got some more caramel going, increasing the cream by 25 grams. The night after next was the first of two friends-and-family nights at Q56, the new hotel restaurant, so I had to have every dessert worked out by then. The caramel bottom for the banana tart Tatin was my only unfinished detail.

With the small taste of success at Scarabée under my belt, I no longer worried whether I could be a pastry chef. Instead, my new focus was to become a *good* pastry chef. I was ready to up my game and take a few chances. I knew I had to have a chocolate dessert, but I was determined not to have the ubiquitous chocolate molten cake that appeared on half of New York City's menus. I didn't care that everyone loved it. It was too easy, too one-note, too obvious. Instead, I decided on a chocolate-espresso custard tart served with "Creamsicle" sherbet, something I thought perfectly fit the definition of "new American cuisine." The small round ball of sherbet would sit on top of the tart in a small crocus-shaped tuile. I made a bright green syrup with basil to give the dessert's flavor a slightly herbal dimension and to add a flash of color. It was a small detail that added a hint of complexity and made the dessert decidedly not humdrum. It was a risk but one I could take, since the rest of my menu consisted of mostly familiar flavors, like the banana tart Tatin. If I could nail down that caramel, I knew the dessert would be a hit. Who doesn't like warm bananas and caramel? Especially served with dark rum ice cream and macadamia nut brittle.

"How's it going, Doll?" said Joey, sauntering through the doorway of my kitchen. *My* kitchen.

Space was a huge perk of working at the hotel. I had an entire room, complete with multiple stainless prep tables, deep sinks, double-decker convection ovens, and a walk-in refrigerator and freezer all to myself. It was a huge improvement over the six feet of basement table space I had at Scarabée. And space was not the only perk that came with working for a large, corporate entity; there was money, too. It was a whole new realm of budgeting.

In addition to a healthy salary increase (finally, I would no longer be living paycheck to paycheck), I was given some great equipment. A few days earlier, after Joey explained the superiority of housemade ice creams and sorbets to the general manager (and spending authority) of the hotel, a brand-new ice cream machine arrived. Making ice cream quickly became my favorite task, and I began experimenting with textures and flavors, ebullient with the creativity it afforded me with my menu. I tried pumpkin with homemade marshmallow, lemon meringue, peppermint stick, prune and Armagnac, even avocado. I was no longer a slave to an ice cream wholesaler's flavor list or to a minuscule household machine.

"It's going okay," I answered Joey. "Just finalizing the banana. Where have you been all day?"

Joey and I had been officially dating for weeks by then, though most of that time had been spent at the hotel, working. We didn't have quite as much time side by side as we did at Scarabée, partly because of the hotel layout and partly because of his new corporate responsibilities. We made a conscious and determined effort to keep our relationship hidden from absolutely everyone, even Frank, the sous-chef who had worked with us at Scarabée. Casual kitchen hookups happen all the time in restaurants, but relationships are more dangerous. If any other employees figured out our secret, there'd be snickering at the very least. Neither one of us wanted anyone to get the idea that I had been hired for any reason other than talent or merit, or that I was getting any special treatment. Maintaining respect was the most important goal.

"Meetings," he answered. "I don't understand how there can be so many meetings, Doll."

He started to make his way from the doorway over to my side of the room but stopped when he was distracted by the small array of stickers that Gilma had left stuck to her side of the table. Technically, Gilma was part of the pastry department, since she was responsible for things like cutting outsourced brownies for corporate events and arranging plates of chocolate-covered strawberries for VIP guests every day. I hated making those chocolate-covered strawberries. What hotel management saw as "luxury" I viewed as mediocre and generic. The out-of-season strawberries were always grossly large with tough, pale flesh. Each one lent little more than slightly sweet juice to the chocolate that coated it. It was one thing I looked forward to improving in the coming months. Gilma also put together shallow bowls of whole fruit for special guests, and every day—every single day—she peeled the small oval stickers off the Red Delicious apples, the underripe bananas and pears, and every single day she stuck them (and left them) on the surface of the table.

"Why does she have to do this, Doll?" Joey started to peel off the small, white ovals from the table. "It's a simple thing. I just want her to stick them into the garbage or on a paper towel or something. I've asked her fifty times, but she just won't do it. It drives me *crazy*."

"She's marking her territory," I offered, shrugging.

Gilma, like most of the employees, had been working there for many years, and had met our arrival and the hotel's decision to revamp and upgrade its restaurant with suspicion. When Joey announced that I'd be using the room to produce in-house desserts and proposed that Gilma use the other side of the table so that I could be on the side closest to the new ovens, she stiffened defiantly, lips pressed firmly into a thin line. She'd moved, but only after Joey had enlisted the cooperation of one of her coworkers, a shop steward in the union who convinced her, begrudgingly, to oblige. To say that Gilma was antagonistic is not exactly accurate, since she barely acknowledged my existence. She mostly pretended that I didn't exist, and I, in turn, counted the minutes until her shift was over at three o'clock every day and the air of hostility dissipated.

Joey picked off all the stickers—he hated any sign of disorder or mess—dropped them into the trash, and finally stood next to me, keeping a few feet of space between us.

"So," I asked, "what kind of meetings did you have?"

"Who even knows? They hand out all these charts with all these numbers. Everyone talks a lot, but no one really says anything. And you know I'm not good at sitting still, Doll."

It was true; he wasn't. It was another reason I'd taken on all computer work. Joey knew everything there was to know about running a restaurant, but sitting through meetings, especially if graphs were involved, was not something he tolerated well.

"All I know," he said finally, leaning victoriously toward me, "is that when it comes down to food cost, I'm always right in line. *Always.*"

Joey prided himself on hitting a food cost of 27 or 28 percent every month, meaning that the ingredients for each dish cost no more than 28 percent of its selling price. Keeping a food cost of below 30 percent is imperative to the financial success of a restaurant, and every percentage point counts.

"You know what I do sometimes when I'm in these meetings?" he asked, taking a tiny step closer. "I rest my head on my hand and rub my fingers through my hair, like this." He demonstrated how, with only his middle finger extended through his hair, he secretly but effectively gave the finger, his own personal "fuck you" to the corporate monster.

I'd been lured (as had Joey) by the challenge of opening a new restaurant, especially one with so much financing and support behind it: The hotel really seemed interested in making a big change with the new restaurant and was willing to spend to ensure its success. It was a challenge in scope, too. I was responsible not just for the restaurant desserts but for room service and private events and even the amenities, the tiny gifts left for guests in the rooms. The pay was better, too, along with the corporate perks like paid vacation, sick days, and personal days, all unheard of in the "outside" world. But I'd only been there a week and Joey a few more, and we'd already grown wary of the corporate entity we'd signed on with. Kitchens were supposed to be the antithesis of the corporate world with its orientations, appearance standards, and endless paperwork. Luckily, I was part of Joey's team. In my mind, I worked for him, not the hotel.

"Nice one," I said, approving of his gesture. He knew more about running a restaurant than anyone in those meetings.

"So, how's the banana?" he asked.

"Okay," I answered. "I'm having a tiny bit of trouble with the caramel, but I think I've just about got it."

"Did I ever tell you, Doll, that the first time I saw you make the pear tarts at Scarabée I was really nervous?"

"What?" I asked. "You were afraid they were gonna suck?"

"A little." He smiled. "But then you flipped that first one over, and all the pear slices had melted into the caramel and it looked beautiful. It was perfect. I knew everything was gonna be great. Just like now."

I smiled. I wanted to put my head on his shoulder or hold his hand or something. Whisper "thank you" in his ear. But I didn't. I couldn't. I just stood there smiling at him.

"Joseph!"

Joey nonchalantly took a step away from me as Carol from marketing stepped into the kitchen waving a stiff piece of paper. Joey had mandated that he be addressed only as Joseph. He thought it sounded more professional and less diminutive, I guess. I still hadn't gotten used to it.

"Joseph!" she said again, excited. "We got the promotional materials in."

We liked Carol, even if she was a suit. She spoke to us as equals and even seemed to understand our disdain for our new corporate identity. And she was genuinely excited about promoting the new restaurant.

"What do you think?" she asked, proudly handing over the large folded card.

On the cover was a stylized close-up of a baby artichoke against a glowing red background. It opened up to another stylized close-up, this time a slightly grainy black-and-white of Joey's—I mean Joseph's—hands plating a salmon tartare with the words *performance* and *art* at the top. A final fold opened up to a full-page sepia photo of four perfectly attractive and diverse but forgettable friends enjoying a meal at Q56. Joseph, the host, stood behind them staring knowingly out at the reader. In the top right corner was the word *energy*. There was copy to the left of the photo, and the Q56 and American Express logos to the right.

"Looks great, Carol," Joey said. I nodded. Clearly a lot of money had gone into its production. Too much, I thought, but I kept my mouth shut.

"The mailing goes out next week," Carol explained. "Every American Express cardholder within a ten-block radius will get one. I think it's really going to get people in here," she said sincerely.

"Well," she said, looking at her watch, "I'm getting out of here. I'll see you guys tomorrow."

"Thanks, Carol," said Joey. "The card looks really great."

"What do you think, Doll?" he asked once Carol was gone.

"Did you get a manicure for that close-up?" I teased. "Because it looks like you got a manicure. Your nails are *not* that shiny in real life."

"Doll," he said, "they *made* me get one! Come on. What do you really think?"

"No, it's good. You look great," I said. It was true. He looked great but still natural, like he did in real life. But Joey knew me too well. I was holding back.

"Come on," he urged. "What is it? I want to know what you really think."

"Well, it's just . . ." I stammered, trying to pinpoint exactly what it was that rubbed me the wrong way. It was those words.

"Performance? Art? Energy?" I said finally. "What is that? It sounds so corny, so . . . ad agency."

I should've just shut up. The hotel *had* spent a lot of money on an ad agency and all the industry trappings—stylists, photographers, and models—to produce promotional materials to get people in the door.

"But honestly, Joey," I said, recovering, "you do look great. And you know what? The food looks amazing, and that's the most important thing. That's why people are going to come here and come back. For the food." I meant every word. Joey's food was undeniably excellent, and I hoped my desserts would leave people wanting more, too.

"I know it's a little cheesy," he agreed. "But this hotel stuff is a whole new ball game. They know what they're doing." He paused before leaning in and lowering his voice. "And," he said devilishly, "I *do* look really good."

I considered this. "The food looks better, though."

"I know," he said, turning to leave, "but only by a hair."

It was after seven and most of the staff was gone, so we had the luxury of being able to joke around. I was reminded of how much I missed the freedom—the enveloping and comfortable banter—we'd enjoyed at Scarabée.

"Doll," Joey said suddenly, looking at his watch and walking back toward me. "Let's get out of here early."

"Really?" I looked at my watch. We usually worked until at least nine.

"Yeah," he said. "You can finish the banana tomorrow. Why don't you pack up your stuff and meet me in twenty minutes? I'll go get the bug and pick you up down the block. We can pick up some sushi and watch a movie or something. It'll probably be the last chance we'll have for a while to take this kind of break."

In order to keep up appearances, we never arrived or left within twenty minutes of each other.

"That sounds perfect." Right after the friends-and-family nights, we'd be open to the public, and there was no telling when we'd get to take a breath. I happily cleaned up my area.

Once inside Joey's baby blue '71 Volkswagen bug, I forgot all about the promotional materials and corporate identities, co-worker façades and menu perfection. I rested my head on Joey's shoulder as we headed downtown.

✦

NINETEEN

Reality Bites

F uck me!"

It was the only thing I could say, my solitary sentiment, as my hand slipped off the edge of the large bain-marie of chocolate sauce I was holding.

"Motherfucker!"

I didn't recover quickly enough, and so the bain fell over. I watched the mass of thick, hot, near-black sauce—a good six quarts—ooze across my table in a slow, steady blob. It blanketed my notebook, which had all my recipes-in-progress, and ran over the edge of the table and onto the floor before I could slow it with a stack of side towels.

"*Hmmph . . .*"

Gilma stared smugly at me from across the room, fixing her

collage of fruit stickers to the table. She made no effort to lend a hand, and I responded to Gilma the way I always responded to Gilma. I ignored her.

Using a week's worth of side towels, I mopped up the sticky chocolate mess and attempted to salvage my notebook. One by one I wiped the pages off with a damp towel. Amazingly, it worked, and I lost only a few minutes cleaning up the disaster. At least I had my notebook and the months of work I'd done on new recipes. I kept meaning to transfer them to the computer.

I grabbed the dirty pot and headed for the pot sink to drop it off but stopped in my tracks a few feet before the sink.

"What are you doing?" I asked, dirty pot still in hand. Three dishwashers were huddled around the pot sink, hunched over a magazine.

I knew what they were doing; I could see the glare of bare skin staring back at me from the large, glossy photos in the porn magazine. The three men just stared at me and my stupid pot, looking irritated that I'd interrupted them and, even worse, that I'd dared to question them.

What began as an exciting opportunity to open a new restaurant had slowly turned into a borderline unbearable situation. The day-to-day minutiae of kitchen work had proved to be frustrating to the point of complete exasperation. The "old" employees did little to help the "new" and sometimes even went out of their way to make our lives more difficult. In a normal restaurant, the chef reigns, and each person works to support everyone else to make everything run smoothly, like a well-oiled machine. But that spirit of cooperation was lost at Q56. It was not a normal restaurant; it was a corporate one with a union staff—a different animal entirely.

"I need this pot, please," I said, at least trying to sound authoritative.

Not only did they meet my request with a collective eye roll, but they didn't even bother hiding their porn. I considered repeating the policy I'd been taught at orientation that imposed a ban on all pornographic material in the workplace and forbade any form of sexual harassment, but I had a feeling it would just elicit more eye rolls. *What?* I wanted to yell at them. *Like you're gonna jerk off between pots? All three of you together?* The group consumption of porn was weird enough, but in the workplace? I wished I could intimidate them or even humiliate them, but I knew it would be useless. It wasn't the porn that offended me so much—working in kitchens, I'd been privy to plenty of raunchy, locker-room chat from the many men I'd worked with—it was their complete lack of respect for my supposed authority (I was in a management position, after all) and for the restaurant that I wanted so desperately to succeed. I dropped off the pot and went back to my kitchen.

Maybe I was just tired. I had worked thirty-three straight days, every one of them a double, and the daily battles, small as they sometimes were, were beginning to take their toll.

Back in the pastry kitchen, Gilma had finished her fruit bowls and left her daily sticker arrangement on the table as always. I wanted to shove her out of the way and pick them off, show her how easy it would be. As if ease had anything to do with it. I started weighing out the *mise-en-place* for chocolate sauce attempt number two.

"Dalia!" said Evelyn, one of the good waiters, one of the few who had been trying her best to keep up with all the new food and upgrades in service and wine. There were a few cooks, too, whom Joey had hired who gave us some respite from the antagonistic old regime. These cooks had come to work for Joey, not the hotel, and they gave us hope that the restaurant might have a chance. "There's someone here to see Joseph."

"Okay," I told her. "I'll be right out."

The staff had certainly realized that Joey and I were close. If they couldn't find him they usually came to me, figuring that I'd either know where he was or that I'd know the answer to a given question or problem. As far as I could tell, though, we'd been successful in keeping our secret. In fact, keeping the secret had turned out to be easier than actually maintaining the relationship.

Our personal and private lives had become so completely entwined that it was hard to tell where one ended and the other began: Joseph-my-boss and Joey-my-boyfriend were virtually one and the same. Hiding my feelings at work was easy, since most of the time at work I felt frustrated and stressed, not loving and romantic, which left little opportunity for an affectionate glance or tender moment to slip out. By the time we got home late at night, we were too tired for anything but sleep, after which we got up early and started all over again.

I watched Evelyn walk back to the podium to see who was waiting for Joey. When I finally saw her, my stomach began to contract with nausea. Ohhh nooo . . . Camille. French coat-check Camille from Scarabée. Fucking stupid, hot, tight-pants-wearing, perfect-ass Camille. What was she doing here? I thought she'd gone back to France.

I didn't want to deal with her; in fact, I didn't feel physically able to deal with her. I had a quick look around, scanning for Joey, but I didn't see him. He could have been anywhere: in a meeting, in the basement. He often slipped away, finding brief respite in the second-floor conference rooms or downstairs in the gym. Even if I had seen him, my torso was filling up so quickly with bile that I might have simply spit when informing him that she was waiting. In *my* workplace. Why the fuck was she here?

Seeing her, with her dirty blond hair pulled up in high pigtail braids, eyebrows raised expectantly, and, yes, tight pants, I was suddenly and absolutely overwhelmed with regret. Regret for falling for Joey, regret for dating him while under the pressure of opening this stupid restaurant, regret for not being able to hold myself together because some stupid girl he used to date had turned up where I work. Suddenly, I hated my job: Gilma, the pot washers, hotel management, human resources, all of it. As I walked through the dining room to the podium, I hated the cool and happy instrumental music, too. All the money the hotel had blown on "music consultants" to create the perfect vibe, and we ended up sounding like a goddamn Banana Republic commercial.

"Hi, Camille," I said dryly, holding it together.

"Ello, Dal-ee-ah," she said cheerfully in her youthful, thick French accent. "I was looking for Joey? Eeez he here?" She craned her head, looking past me.

I realized that she must not know about me and Joey . . . or did she? My stomach hardened as I considered for a moment that maybe I had been taken for a fool, that this little dingbat Frenchie knew very well where I stood with Joey but simply chose to ignore it, and that Joey had betrayed me. My eyes glazed over, and my jaw stiffened.

"Um," I said vaguely, "I don't know where he is right now. Somewhere in the building . . ."

She just stood there, smiling like a dummy. "Okay. I'll wait."

Okay, I'll wait? Who did she think she was? This was where I worked, a supposed high-end restaurant, not some slacker café where she could just laze around for hours. I rushed back through the dining room and into the kitchen, determined to find Joey, to get answers, to make him get rid of her. I felt like my home, broken though it may have been, was being occupied by a foreign invader.

As I rushed through the kitchen, I caught a waiter putting some rolls into a microwave. "What are you doing?" I almost yelled.

"Some lady wants warm bread." Greg shrugged, hitting the buttons. *Beep beep beep.* Greg had been a waiter at the hotel for years, despite his rumored problem with crystal meth. He was almost never pleasant and had a twitching, sour face. He'd been offered a buyout—a lump sum payment in exchange for "early retirement"—as had some of the other undesirable but tenured waiters, but had refused.

"You don't microwave bread," I spit out, opening the microwave door and pulling out the rolls. "It'll turn hard as a rock as soon as it cools. Just give it to one of the cooks to warm up in the oven. It'll take two seconds."

"Yeah," he said under his breath, taking the sizzle platter of bread out of my hand. "Like it matters."

"It *does* matter," I yelled back, knowing full well that as soon as my back was turned he'd be back to his old ways. But it did matter. Why didn't anyone fucking think it mattered? I walked away, not caring that I'd made him the object of my anger, of my feeling of being trapped—in more ways than one—by the four walls of the hotel.

I started my search for Joey downstairs in the purchaser's office. Nothing. Storage, prep kitchen, office. Nothing, nothing, nothing. I was storming, actually storming, by the time I found him coming down the stairs in the hallway near our office.

"Joey!" I called. He stopped at the bottom of the stairs.

"What is it, Doll? What's wrong?"

"Have you been seeing Camille?" I asked, keeping my face as stony as could be. As if nonchalance were even a remote possibility.

"Camille?" he asked, confused. "What are you talking about? No, why?"

"She's here," I said sternly. "Why is she here?"

"Doll," he said, sensing I was on the brink. "Let's go into the office."

"I don't know why she's here," he said once the door was closed behind us.

The sudden privacy knocked me over the edge, and before I

knew it I was regrettably and totally in tears. All of the pressure that had been building up over the past months was forcing its way out, and I couldn't help becoming emotional. I could no longer pretend that our relationship didn't exist.

"I just don't understand why she's here," I sobbed. "And why doesn't she know about us? She wouldn't come by if she thought you were unavailable."

Joey let me sit and cry for a minute, releasing my worst fears, my aggravation and frustration. In the midst of my tears I also felt guilty for having laid all this on him and for letting my personal life interfere with my professional one. Our relationship had become so complicated.

"Doll," he said, putting his arm around me, keeping one eye on the closed door just in case someone walked in. "I haven't seen her in months. She must have heard I was working here."

I looked at him, horrified that I'd become a blubbering fool in an oversized chef's coat stained with chocolate sauce.

"Think about it, Doll," he went on. "When would I have seen her? I'm with you every day and every night."

He had a very good point. I had failed to remember that.

"She's waiting outside for you. Can't you just go tell her about us so at least she won't come back to where we work?"

"I'll get rid of her, but you know I can't tell her about us now, not here. Too many people around." He handed me a tissue and headed out the door. He was right. I knew he was right. He couldn't have any sort of scene at the restaurant, and who knew how she might react, but I still hated the situation. No matter what happened, I tried to reassure myself, it was just one job of many, and it wouldn't last forever.

It wasn't long after the whole Camille incident that things went from bad to worse. After spending so much energy keeping our relationship out of our work, we had little success keeping work out of our relationship. Joey and I had both become so stressed, so tired, that by the end of the day, we had little to give each other in the way of support. Eventually, the only thing holding us together was work; we were dating by default. By the time I met Les (a photo editor blessedly far removed from the restaurant world) at a party and was instantly attracted, it was simply the final nail in the proverbial coffin. The time had come for my romantic relationship with Joey to be absolutely and undeniably over.

It was a relatively painless split and a relief for both of us, I think. No more breakdowns for me, no more late nights at work wishing I could just go to dinner and a movie with my boyfriend like everyone else. No more contemplating the complexities of a relationship in which pleasing my boss (and living up to his expectations) meant pleasing my boyfriend and vice versa.

Amazingly, we managed to salvage our superlative work relationship, though at a greater distance and with fewer private jokes and glances. Joey pretended not to be bothered when Les called, and I pretended that I didn't care that he was sleeping with the newest restaurant manager, the one who wore dresses and high heels to work every day. The one who, unlike me, always looked pretty at work. We settled into a tolerable rhythm; most of the enmity between us and the worst of the employees had faded to indifference. We focused instead on the few cooks who actually cared. There was Jimmy, the loudmouth cook in his twenties who still lived with his mother. Jimmy wanted so badly to do well that he actually cried when Joey sent him off the line for not listening. We loved Charlotte, the more experienced cook who had been a chef in her own right but at lower-end establishments. She wanted to hone her skills with higher-end food and quickly devoted herself to Joey. There was Hon Lee, my Chinese-American assistant, who became known as anything but Hon Lee: Hon Solo, Crème Hon Glaise, Honda, Honshimeji. We wondered about Diana, the career changer who came to work with perfectly coifed hair, three pounds of makeup caked on, and professional manicures. She didn't last long, but a few others did and were invaluable, as much for keeping our spirits up as for their cooking skills. We still had the restaurant to run (even if business hadn't picked up), the employees to deal with, the food to prepare, and, we thought, a *Times* review to await.

But it was taking too long. Normally, a new restaurant, especially one with money, a hefty PR firm, and a name chef behind it, got reviewed within the first few months of opening. And we were ready. We had photos of the new *Times* critic (sadly the previous one who had raved about Joey's food at Scarabée had since left the paper), along with some of his aliases and phone numbers. Months passed without a visit from the critic, but I still had hope that he would come. Until the phone rang one night at work.

"Doll?"

The hotel kitchen line I'd picked up was inconveniently located near the room service kitchen throughway, so I could hardly hear the warbled and weak voice on the other end of the line. The voice was familiar, though. And only one person would have called me Doll over the phone.

"Joey?" I asked. "Is that you?" I put my free hand over my other ear to block out the distractions.

"Yeah, Doll," he said. "It's me."

Why was he calling me? Since breaking up, we'd limited our interaction to work-related stuff; no more late-night chats, no nightcaps, definitely no overnights. It was only seven thirty, so he should have been in the kitchen expediting dinner service. I could tell by the type of ring that he was calling from outside the building. It sounded like he'd been crying.

"Where are you?" I asked.

"Doll," he said after a long pause. "I got some bad news."

My chest tightened as I suddenly panicked that something terrible had happened to someone in his family. I dismissed any definitions and parameters of our ever-changing relationship. I didn't care what our status was; I just wanted to be there for him.

"What is it, Joey? What happened?"

He was quiet for a long time, gathering his voice.

"Doll, I talked to Steven," he said, pausing again. "We're not getting reviewed." He let the receiver fall away from his head.

I allowed myself a brief moment of relief—no one was hurt or in danger—before I began to understand the gravity of the information. Steven was our public relations guy, our interface with the press. Though he had no real power over what actually got written, a large part of his job was to convince writers and critics that we were worth a visit and hopefully a review.

Joey was talking about *the* review, the only one that really mattered—the *New York Times*. The one that validated all the hard work. The one that made it all worth it. If we weren't getting a *Times* review *and* business wasn't picking up on its own, then what were we working for?

It wasn't as though we hadn't gotten *any* press since opening. Joey's food had been lauded but mostly in smaller publications. It was my desserts that received the lion's share of press: They had been photographed for countless magazines and newspapers, thanks to our PR firm. I'd been featured in local newspapers across the country after being included in an Associated Press article on custards, and I even had my first brush with "the public," if that's what you call a creepy guy calling from Somewhere, California, who complimented me for looking cute on the front page of his town's paper. My ice creams appeared in the *New York Times* and in a spread on dessert cocktails in *New York* magazine, among others. I was even on television when a Japanese morning show decided to feature one of my desserts. Though I'd been prepped for the questions beforehand (I was interviewed briefly through a translator), I realized after watching it that my future probably didn't lie in television. Still, the attention I received for my work had been good for my ego. But none of this brought people rushing through the doors of Q56, because, let's face it, people just don't flock to restaurants just for the desserts. Especially not hotel restaurants in midtown. Hearing the defeat in Joey's voice made all of my own press infinitely superfluous. I would have traded it all in for a single *Times* review.

"I'm not coming back in tonight, Doll," he said before I could respond. "Tell Frank I had something to take care of."

Frank was more than capable of taking charge of the kitchen, especially since we'd been so slow. I wished Joey were taking a much-needed night off under better circumstances. I wished I could do something.

"Of course," I said.

"Doll," he added, straining. "Can you come over?"

Come over. It wouldn't be like old times. I glanced at my watch, though there was no question about my answer.

"Sure," I said. "Let me just finish up, and I'll be right there."

It felt strange to be heading downtown to Joey's place again. I knew Joey well enough to know he probably hadn't eaten all day and wouldn't have any food in his apartment, so I picked up some comfort junk food on the way: nachos and Chubby Hubby ice cream, his favorite. When I reached his fourth-floor walk-up after being buzzed in, the door was slightly ajar. The apartment was dark, except for the shimmering, iridescent light of the television, its volume barely audible. I pushed the door open and found Joey hunched over the end of the couch, his head resting on the arm.

"Hi, Doll," he said, barely lifting his head.

"Hi."

I took my coat off and dropped the junk food on the coffee table.

"I thought you might be hungry," I offered.

"Thanks, Doll." He opened the nachos, crunched, and then sighed as if it were the first breath he'd taken in a while.

"So what happened?" I finally asked, sitting down next to him. I wanted details.

"I talked to Steven," he said slowly, as if the pain were still fresh.

"Yeah," I coaxed.

"And he talked to him. Asked him what was going on, when he was gonna come in, review us." He paused. "He said he'd been in once for lunch and decided not to come back." He paused again. "He said"—Joey's voice became strained and his face stony before he finished—"that we weren't *memorable.*"

Joey buried his head in the sofa arm again, reliving the news. And the pain.

"I'm not memorable, Doll," he sobbed. "I'm nothing. Not even worth a review. That's what he thinks."

For as long as I'd known him, and on all the different levels, Joey had been a pillar of strength, the person in charge, able to handle any situation, confidently take care of anyone and anything. But after having his talent and integrity questioned and, even worse, dismissed, he was wounded. It killed me to see him in pain, but it was remotely comforting to know that he was human, too. I reached over and put my arms around him. In spite of everything, or maybe because of it, he was still my best friend. I didn't really know what to say.

"He probably wasn't talking about the food, Joey," I offered, trying to take the focus off him. "After all, it is a *restaurant* review; it covers the whole experience, not just the food. Maybe he just didn't like the whole hotel vibe thing."

It was very likely; Q56 had little charm. For all the money that had been spent on its design, the room still felt utterly and inescapably like a hotel dining room, with none of the "slick and sexy" vibe the hotel had hoped for. The lobby was visible from the bar, and one of the head bartenders was Josephine, a dowdy gray-haired woman who looked to be in her sixties and who rarely smiled as she wobbled behind the bar in her updated uniform. The music remained a disaster. Overall, the service barely made it past mediocre. Human resources repeatedly hired managers with little experience outside of the hotel world.

"Yeah, but still," he countered with defeat, "whatever he ate wasn't good enough to make up for any of that."

"But imagine a worst-case scenario, Joey. Maybe he came in, and no one was at the podium to seat him. And then maybe his waiter was Sam, who almost goes out of his way to be rude. And then no one brought him bread. Or water. Or the glass of wine he ordered. And maybe the crappy soundtrack grated on him. Maybe that's what happened. Clearly no one spotted him, or we would have known he'd been in." I was pouring salt in the wound by bringing up the last bit, reminding him of an earlier incident.

At our friends-and-family night, the general manager—the *general manager!*—had turned away an important food critic from *New York* magazine. The GM was new to the nonhotel restaurant scene and hadn't recognized her. *Sorry,* he told her, *but it's too late to be seated.* She, in turn, angrily reported the exchange to Steven. Upon learning that she'd been turned away, Joey called the hotel bigwigs together and voiced his anger and frustration with their inability to understand or heed all the things he'd been trying to tell them. They'd let down their end of the bargain, not Joey. I desperately wanted to take the failure off of Joey's shoulders and place it firmly in the hands of the hotel, where it belonged. I wanted it to be their fault. They deserved it. I started to get angry.

"Joey, you've done everything you could have possibly done," I finally said. "And anyway, I don't care what the guy *said.* He can say anything he wants, but I know, *I know* that your food is delicious and amazing and very memorable. And you know it, too."

He nodded unconvincingly into the sofa.

"But what are we going to do, Doll?" he finally said after a long pause.

What were we going to do? Without a positive review from the *Times,* it was likely Q56 would never get any busier. It was quite possible that the restaurant would slip further and further into midtown hotel obscurity. The hotel would still have its restaurant, which would really exist only to serve its guests, and we'd still have our jobs and the frustrating reality that we were unable to change things.

"I don't know, Joey. I guess we just keep making the best food we can, right?" I said. "And we figure something out."

Eventually, Joey bounced back, determined not to let the *Times* or the hotel defeat him. We did the best job we could until finally none of it seemed worth it to any of us. We'd made it a year when we decided that we could leave our jobs in good conscience. Once again, we left: Joey, Frank, and I, together.

❖

TWENTY

Sweet Relief

After leaving Q56, I worked part-time for Moomba, a celebrity hot spot that had recently turned mostly lukewarm. Moomba's pastry chef had left, so they hired me to maintain the *mise-en-place* for the desserts. I worked just three days a week, mostly on my own, since the restaurant was closed for lunch. On the heels of the antagonistic atmosphere at the hotel, the solitude and silence were bliss, as was the low stress level. I was not expected to come up with anything new; I simply had to maintain what was already in place. It paid enough to cover my rent and gave me a much-needed break. I even took a vacation: a four-week trip to the Philippines and Thailand with Les.

I wasn't counting on Joey to find me my next job (in fact, leaving Q56 gave me a much-needed break from Joey, too), but when

I heard his voice on my answering machine once again—*Gimme a buzz, Doll. I got something to talk to you about.*—I knew he had something in the works. While I was off in Asia, Joey had signed on to be the new chef at Tonic, a restaurant and private party space that had opened a few years earlier. Tonic had received a glowing two stars from the *Times* early on, but its chef was moving on to another project (as chefs tend to do). The owner, Steve, a Greek man in his early sixties who had been in the business for years and owned a handful of restaurants, wanted to breathe some new life into Tonic, whose business had begun to wane. Joey got his team—me and Frank—back together for the job. He even hired some of the better cooks he'd hired at the hotel.

At both Scarabée and Q56, Joey hired me as his pastry chef with no contest from owners or management; they simply trusted his judgment. This time, though, Joey's word on my behalf was not enough for Steve. I was asked to do a tasting: prepare some of my desserts so he could get a realistic idea of what I would serve in his restaurant. The taste, the style, the look—all of these things would be judged.

I needed surefire desserts (trying out new things was too risky), so I stuck to things I'd done before: banana tarte Tatin, milk chocolate pot de crème, lemon blast (a frozen lemon soufflé). I brought each plate out to Steve, his wife, and Joey, who sat with them, as though he were part of the judging panel. I described each dessert as I imagined it would appear on a menu: *This is the lemon blast, with blueberry frozen yogurt and vanilla shortbread.* Then, I retreated down to the basement to work on the next one, happy not to have to face their reactions, their critique. That I had complete faith in my desserts (as did Joey) was no guarantee and of little comfort. People have different tastes, and, for all I knew, Steve might have hated the hint of whimsy in my lemon blast: It was an oval frozen soufflé that had a peephole cut through one end, on which I leaned a small, round scoop of frozen yogurt. I decorated the plate with a swirl of sauces. The other restaurants in Steve's small empire were more traditional. Maybe he would think it was stupid. Conversely, maybe he wanted something outrageous, like the towering, architectural, overgarnished look that was popular in some high-end restaurants. I found that the taste of those desserts rarely lived up to their visual spectacle, but some customers loved them nonetheless.

But Steve did like my desserts. His only question, Joey told me later, was a trivial one. *The girl,* he asked Joey, *does she know how to use the machine?* I was twenty-nine at the time, far too old to be thought of as a girl, even if I did still look like one. I hated that my appearance could undermine my ability or talent, but at least I had Joey to back me up. He assured Steve that not only could I use the ice cream machine, but I had plenty of high-volume experience to handle the production necessary for Tonic's two private rooms, which could hold up to two hundred people. I was in and determined to prove myself to be much more than just "the girl."

Working at Tonic meant a return to "normal" restaurant life: We worked six-day weeks, shared family meals, and spent too much time together. Tonic had a pretty big staff (though still significantly smaller than that of the hotel), which consisted of the usual hodgepodge of personalities who managed, despite their differences, to get along and joke around.

Working in such close quarters and with mostly young men encouraged sophomoric humor. I always stored my tart shells in the same place: bottom shelf of my walk-in refrigerator. Quite regularly I would grab the plastic-wrapped half sheet tray and realize that something was different. My handwritten, blue ink labeling had been altered. My *T* for "tart" had been turned into an *F*. Again. Using words for body parts or body functions was considered hysterically funny: *butt* as in *butt milk* for "buttermilk" or *box* for "refrigerator." If a body part, especially a private body part, could in any way be substituted for a kitchen word, it was. *Fart* was the funniest at all times and in any application. Any sound resembling a fart? Also funny. For instance, squeezing the last bit of honey out of its bottle so it made a spitting noise. Blaming someone for it with a chorus of accusing *eeews*? Very funny. Turning the pastry chef's tart into a fart? It didn't get any better.

Thanks to my French predecessor, who had designed the pastry station (he was less than pleased to learn that he was being replaced by a "girl"), my area was a dream; it was well equipped and well organized. I had my own end of the basement kitchen, complete with double convection oven, sink, burners, lowboys, mixers, and freezers. I even had a lot of "pastry-only" equipment—chinois, Robo Coupe, blender—which meant that my desserts could not be mistakenly adulterated by some other cook's garlic or fish stock. There is nothing worse than innocently puréeing some fruit in a Robo Coupe only to discover, too late, that it tastes like the garlic that has stubbornly sunk into the plastic body of the food processor. There was plenty of space for both me and Ali, my assistant, who came in every day at two and worked until closing.

When I started at Tonic, Ali had been a dishwasher and a good one (being a dishwasher is hard work and a good one should not be taken for granted), but whenever he had a free moment, he would stand at the edge of my station, watching intently as I arranged berries on a tart, spread out tuile batter over a stencil, or scooped cookie dough. After a while, if I was doing a simple task, topping hundreds of miniature pistachio cakes with a single whole Sicilian pistachio, for example, I would ask him if he wanted to help, and he always nodded. He worked diligently and quietly, barely looking me in the eye. When my nighttime plater (the very job I'd had at Nobu so long ago) quit, I offered Ali the job.

It was rough going at first. Ali was from Mali and spoke both Arabic and French. His English, however, was only as good as my spotty French. But Ali always carried a small notebook in which he recorded everything I taught him. With naturally deft hands, he easily rolled out even logs of biscotti dough, and his tuiles were always thin and uniform. When his plates looked a little bit sloppy or just plain wrong, I tried to be patient, remembering how horrendous my own fruit plates and "Happy Birthdays" had been at Nobu when I first started. And just as I had improved over time and with repetition, Ali improved exponentially. I eventually learned to trust him completely. Not only did Ali become an amazing assistant, he started taking English classes and even earned his green card. Eventually, he arrived at work one day with a new identification card complete with his given name in an African dialect. We "fired" the old illegal Ali and "hired" the new legal one, the one with a name none of us could come close to pronouncing. *It's okay,* he said, *you can still call me Ali.*

Watching Ali grow in so many ways was wonderful, and I liked to believe that I played a tiny part in his achievement, but he was more likely inspired by some of the other cooks around him. It is not uncommon for a dishwasher, the lowest position in a kitchen, to gradually work his way up through the hierarchy until finally becoming a chef. It is one of the aspects of kitchens I like the best: They are great equalizers. Hard work and diligence pay off, regardless of class, race, or school transcripts.

Part of Ali's daily responsibility was steadily laying out tuile batter over the thin plastic stencils I'd cut out of old plastic fish tubs. Over time, he did just as good a job as I did. Once he mastered something, I taught him something new, building on his skills. Ali and I fell into a routine: He came in every day and prepped the station for dinner service, and I spent the bulk of my time producing the more complicated items and coming up with new ideas. It was not until I finally relaxed into the more normal and supportive environment of Tonic that I realized how much the frustration and stress of the hotel had affected my outlook. I had forgotten how much I loved creating desserts and even working in a restaurant.

Q56 had been a disaster, but the desserts I developed there were not, so many of them reappeared on my Tonic menu. I kept the buttermilk crème brûlée and served it this time with miniature blueberry scones. The brûlée was so popular that I baked them almost every other day, which should have meant that I could not only bake them in my sleep but bake a batch without burning myself. But burns remained a constant though less frequent fact of my life. I was checking on my buttermilk crème brûlées one afternoon as they baked in my top convection oven. They were reaching that critical stage: nearing the point at which they would obtain that exact and perfect wiggle, not unlike Jell-O, that indicated doneness. A few too many minutes past that point and the small white ramekins of custard would be rendered useless, pots of sweet, scrambled egg.

I'm short. So short, in fact, that I needed to balance on the tippy toes of my kitchen clogs, Michael Jackson style, to get a glimpse of them on the top rack.

I balanced on my toes, craning my neck toward the crème brûlées to make a proper assessment. My eyes were trained on them as I nudged the pan to check for that wiggle, my depth perception thrown off as I focused more on my desserts than on the hot rack, getting closer and closer until finally the hot oven rack and I shared a quick kiss.

"Crap," I hissed, pulling away from the rack.

By that time I'd burned myself so many times that I could easily judge the impending severity and outcome of any number of different burns. Just-boiled milk spilled on the delicate top skin of the foot? Redness, possible blister (luckily, I was wearing thick socks on the day that happened). Hot oil splattered onto the forearm after I'd dropped an order of fries into the fryer? In addition to a Jackson Pollack–style pattern of burn marks, there would be an annoying throb every time the newly tender area came within a few inches of heat. Happily, I spent far less time over the fryer since becoming a pastry chef, though I often got roped into helping the hot line when they were short staffed. Accidentally placing a palm on the freshly burned sugar of a crème brûlée? Palm-sized, caramel-coated, thick-skinned blister that renders that hand temporarily useless. Bumping mouth into a 300-degree oven while checking crème brûlées? Redness, potential blister, and, of course, embarrassment. I knew what was coming.

"Doll," Charlotte, the daytime sous-chef, asked, feigning sincerity. "You got a herpes sore?"

Charlotte was one of the Q56 cooks who had followed Joey to the Tonic, and it wasn't until she landed at Tonic that I really got to know her, once I finally let go of the thick layer of skin I had developed at the hotel. Charlotte was a good cook and a very hard worker. She had a tendency to talk—and tease—as tough as she worked. Normally she chose the waiters to torment and even bragged about making at least one waiter cry each day when she'd been the chef at a well-known pub downtown.

"Who you been kissing, Doll?" she said again.

I went into the office to look in the mirror we kept there. Joey was obsessive about checking his teeth. He swore the best advice he'd ever given me was to check both my teeth and my shoes for food remnants before going out to a table in the dining room.

"Don't go into the dining room, Doll," Joey said, standing behind me. "You might take someone out with that thing." By this time, Joey had become more like a big brother than an ex-boyfriend or even a boss.

Even Ali, quiet, doe-eyed Ali, who had been working at the counter behind me, hadn't been able to hold back a smirk after hearing me whisper "Crap!" as my lip met the heat of the oven rack.

I'd had more than my fair share of burns, so I knew that the teasing, especially in response to carelessness, was as predictable as the blister itself and there was little I could do in the way of defense. Part of working in a kitchen with a "family" meant accepting the good-humored ribbing that permeated every moment and every aspect of the workday. "We tease because we love" was our mantra, and nothing was sacred, certainly not burns. I deserved a little teasing, and I took it all in stride. I was happy to be back in a restaurant where family meant something.

✦

TWENTY-ONE

More Than Food Alone

Like the rest of New York City, I'd been paralyzed on the morning of September 11, numbed by hours spent in front of the television watching the two planes stab our city straight through its heart over and over in the worst-ever instant replay. I'd overslept, so instead of hearing the news while working in my basement pastry kitchen, I was home, unable to believe my eyes. Twenty-four hours after the crashes, I returned to work at the restaurant with the rest of the kitchen staff. We were unable to get back to our routine and not just because of logistical difficulties (problems with deliveries and reservation cancellations); we were all stunned, our normal motivation paralyzed by the feeling that we should be *doing* something, anything, to help stitch up the city. There was no point in prepping for lunch or dinner service;

few, if any, people would be dining with us that day. Instead, we began to think about the hundreds of people working nonstop downtown who would need to eat. Whatever food they already had would probably be prepackaged, neither fresh nor appetizing. We knew that, even with minimal ingredients, we had the know-how, experience, and, most important of all, the time and resources at that moment to prepare *good* food. We went through all our walk-in boxes and pulled out anything that could be made into a tasty and easily transportable meal. We made as many sandwiches as we could, trying to imagine what the rescue workers would like. We rolled the dough I had proofing in the refrigerator (meant for dinner rolls) into thin discs and then baked them into pita-style rounds that we used for sandwich wraps. We grilled chicken and hanger steak, sliced tomatoes and red onions, mixed mustard sauces and mayonnaises. I baked all the chocolate chip cookie and coconut macaroon batter I had left, hoping it wouldn't seem silly to bring cookies. We loaded everything, along with cases of water, into our restaurant's Jeep.

Our friends and former colleagues at Tribeca Grill, who had been forced to close (since no regular traffic was allowed below Fourteenth Street), had had the same idea. They set up a temporary resting place for relief workers in their dining room, which became a general stopping-off point below Fourteenth Street. A police captain from the neighborhood came out of retirement temporarily to help out his old precinct. When I worked in the neighborhood years earlier, this same captain had been notorious for showing up at restaurants and expecting special attention or service (a burger, even though there wasn't one on the menu, things like that), but with his precinct in need, he shed his air of entitlement. In the days to come, he provided us with the police escort we needed to get past the many protective blockades that surrounded lower Manhattan, and I was reminded of what my father had always said about disasters and wars: Despite their horror, they bring out the best in people.

South of Franklin Street, nonmilitary vehicles were banned altogether, so the only way to get around was on foot. The four of us who had piled into the Jeep loaded up our arms with as much as we could manage and started walking. Instinctively, we each walked alone; to have the safety or comfort of a coworker by our sides seemed an unfair luxury, or maybe we just wanted, or needed, to be alone in the exodus downtown.

I walked first to Stuyvesant High School, where a Red Cross worker told me that the streets farther south would be blocked off and guarded by military. *Try to get past them,* she'd said. *Nothing's getting down that far, and they're desperate.* So I followed her directions and continued south on Greenwich Street, my arms full of food and bottled water, until I reached the line of military trucks and personnel dressed in full camouflage who were protecting the disaster site from any unauthorized or unnecessary visitors. I was not officially authorized; I was just a pastry chef who, along with some coworkers, had acted on a primal need to do something, anything, to help the relief effort going on in the financial district. I approached a man thick with muscles who seemed to be controlling the flow of traffic, lowered my protective mask, and repeated what the Red Cross had told me. He looked me over silently before giving me his answer.

"Walk directly there," he said sternly and clearly, his steely eyes barely visible beneath the brim of his camouflaged army cap. "You drop off the food and you come right back. Don't waste time staring, don't get in anyone's way, and watch where you're going."

I nodded, trying not to fixate on the large firearm that hung across his chest, an automatic weapon, I guessed, not that I had any experience whatsoever with those sorts of things. I'd never seen so many guns in one place, let alone been around so many people ready and willing to use them.

"And you report to me, Colonel DePalma, on your way back. Understand?" he demanded.

"Yes," I told him. I understood. "Thank you."

And so I continued through the throng of military, firefighters, and other rescue workers and replaced the protective white felt mask over my mouth. They were larger than life, with their thick protective gear, hard hats, and aptly named fatigues. Looking down at my own uniform of red-and-white-checked, chocolate-stained pants, baggy white chef's coat, and the pink kitchen clogs that Joey had given me for my birthday, I felt absolutely powerless.

Past the military blockade and with a good six blocks still to walk, I stopped to readjust the case of bottled water, boxes of wrapped sandwiches, and freshly baked cookies in my arms. *Good,* the Red Cross woman had told me, when I showed her the cookies, *they need sugar.* My arms were beginning to ache from the load. I kept going, scolding myself for even allowing the indulgence of even the slightest complaint.

I kept walking, through the dust- and debris-filled air, over the ash-covered streets, past the squashed fire trucks and blown-out windows that grew in number with every step as I got closer to the site. I pinched the thin, metal band of my face mask more tightly around my nose so that it would stay put around my mouth, which was quickly becoming wet with sweat beneath its white felt. It didn't protect my eyes, which were forced into a tighter squint with every step. The fallout seeped in through every sense.

I tried not to look anyone in the eyes, not wanting to get in their way, not wanting to see the horror and sadness reflected there. I was just a small woman bringing some food. I felt embarrassed to be sharing the space with people who were risking so much and had lost so much. I just wanted to relieve them of one tiny worry, make their efforts the tiniest bit more bearable.

"You don't have any hot coffee in there, do you?" asked a fireman leaning against a truck on the side of the road, barely nodding in my direction.

I shook my head no, feeling useless again for not anticipating such an obvious need and being unable to provide the one thing he asked for.

"Sandwiches and cookies," I answered, offering my armload.

He took some cookies and said thank you. I should have been thanking him.

I kept walking.

I reached an enormous hole in the sky that was anchored to the ground by a massive tangle of what had been the towers. I followed a partially cleared path to the right while letting the view take me in, amazed at how a complete void in the skyline could make me feel so small. *Don't waste time staring,* I remembered Colonel DePalma say. I pulled myself away from the view and turned instead into the former lobby of a cracked building that had been set up as a makeshift headquarters for medical treatment and other support. Its large, slanted window frames were empty, their shattered panes sharing the floor with exhausted firemen trying to catch a few moments of rest. I crossed the space crowded with IVs, eyewash stations, blank-eyed rescue workers, and Red Cross volunteers, finally reaching a table piled with prepackaged food. A woman took the weight off my arms with authority, asked what business I was from, and thanked me.

"Anything we can do?" I asked.

"What these guys really need is hot food," she said. "*Real* food."

"Okay," I answered. And she was gone, tending to those others who needed her.

I turned back north, keeping my head down, watching where I was going, and trying not to get in anyone's way.

Three days later what began as an instinctual urge by a few cooks had turned into a citywide effort to provide as much food and drink as necessary. The restaurant world and soon after the larger food world came together to offer help in the best way they knew how. Tonic became a headquarters and a coordination center for donation drop-offs above Fourteenth Street, and we were overwhelmed by the generous contributions. Supermarket chains called to ask us for shopping lists and delivered food by the pallet. Within hours of making a single phone call, hundreds of pounds of coffee were delivered, along with a flatbed truck and huge plastic urns in which to deliver the brewed coffee and keep it hot.

Promises were made that the flow would continue as long as necessary. Cooks from all over, some temporarily out of work because their restaurants had been forced to close as a result of the tragedy, others simply with a day off, heard about our efforts and turned up to show support for the rescue workers and also to pay tribute to our lost colleagues from Windows on the World, the restaurant that was at the top of the World Trade Center. Our kitchen was full with the energy of peeling, chopping, blanching, and seasoning, and with the camaraderie born of a common cause. We were no longer cooking for privileged customers or vying for the attention of critics; our craft was reduced to its most basic definition.

Ruth Reichl, former *New York Times* restaurant critic and now editor in chief of *Gourmet* magazine, joined in, delivering buckets of beef stew that she and her staff made at *Gourmet's* test kitchen. The tables were turned, and for the first time chefs had an opportunity to be on an even playing field with the woman whose words they had for many years feared would make or break them. As soon as she pulled away, someone was opening the lid and taking a sniff.

"Hey!" he called everyone over. "Let's taste her stew."

The cooks and chefs followed, happy for the role reversal.

"*Hmmm,* I don't know," said one, smiling, chewing on a piece of meat. "It's a bit tough!"

"Yeah," said another gleefully, though unconvincingly, "and it needs a bit more seasoning, don't you think?"

"One star!" announced another, closing the lid, as they all looked at each other with satisfaction.

My heart ached when an elderly woman who had heard about our efforts rolled her cart up to the restaurant and handed me dozens of individually wrapped peanut butter sandwiches she'd made.

Disappointment came, too, when one high-profile chef began showing up to help only when the news cameras were rolling, taking much of the credit and using the situation to his own public relations advantage. When the very same chef requested that he be sent only "*fresh* meat and produce" with which to prepare donated food, the restaurant world rolled its collective eyes. He was certainly not the only opportunist during that time. Other chefs and owners became more generous when national television became interested in what we had started. Even sadder were the stories of those who abused Red Cross subsidies, monies that were meant to compensate restaurants near the site for their efforts to continue feeding the relief workers.

We stopped laughing and gossiping when the Red Cross called, advising us to avoid preparing food that contained bones, because it might too closely resemble parts found on site. They said to avoid red sauces, too, because the workers had seen too much blood already. We were reminded that our own priorities should remain focused on getting the necessary food down where it was needed. After more than a few urgent late-night requests for ice, which was needed to keep body parts cold, we loaded our truck with as many ice-filled trash bags as would fit, and drove quietly downtown again.

After those first couple of days, the modest relief effort we began at Tonic grew into a massive tristate endeavor that was centralized downtown, closer to where help was needed. A barge on the Hudson River became the new headquarters, solving the problem of both traffic and space. Restaurants reopened, though some never recovered from the extended forced closings and the loss of foot traffic. We at Tonic, along with the rest of the city, tried to get back to normal.

✤

TWENTY-TWO

A Matter of Taste

Not long after 9/11, Joey received the *New York Times* review that he had so sorely missed at Q56 and with it redemption from the critic who had once deemed Joey, at least in Joey's mind, "not memorable." And the review could not have been better: Bill Grimes raved about Joey's food as well as the beautiful, relaxed dining room and service. He even called my Kalamansi Colada, a layered parfait of coconut sorbet, pink tapioca, and kalamansi (a citrus fruit I discovered while traveling in the Philippines) granita, a "dreamsicle." He mentioned me by name and pointed out other highlights on my menu, the banana tarte Tatin and my carrot cake.

In a marked reversal from a few years earlier, I was able to shrug off his negative comments: that my buttermilk crème brûlée was no better than a thousand others and that my "Stars & Stripes" (mascarpone panna cotta decorated with pomegranate gelée "stars" and a concord grape "stripe") was disorganized and messy. He'd said too many great things about the restaurant, Joey, and my desserts for me to worry about a few negatives. Ironically, the paper called a week later. Grimes was doing a story on patriotic desserts, and, as a result, my "disorganized" dessert ended up being featured in his article. Soon after, other magazines and papers were calling so that they, too, could feature the dessert.

We all heaved a huge sigh of relief: We were part of a critically successful restaurant that was doing well financially. After so many years of working jobs that took over my life, I could finally settle into normalcy. My job was now only part of my life: I worked only five days a week, and only one of those days was a double. I actually had a life. I had time for socializing, dating, cooking for fun, sometimes all at the same time.

I started throwing dinner parties. In a city like New York, where kitchens are afterthoughts, refrigerators have space for little more than ketchup and leftover Chinese, and most people have far more takeout menus than cookbooks, I found that my friends were more than happy to crowd around my living room coffee table (no room for diners in my tiny kitchen and I certainly didn't have a dining room or even a dining table) for a home-cooked meal. My ability to cook was a real asset to my social life, and I used it shamelessly.

When I discovered that Matt, a British writer I began dating, had an endless love for all desserts, or "puddings" as he called them, I took full advantage. When I learned that his favorite ice cream was coffee chip I made it for the restaurant, just so I could bring him a pint the next time we watched a movie at his place. His eyes had widened with excitement at my gift. *It's chock-a-block!* he gushed before gulping it down. He devoured every little cake, cookie, and candy with boyish glee.

Even so, when Matt asked me to help him cook a dinner for his friends, I was a bit apprehensive. I knew he wanted to show off both his own abilities and mine (dating a pastry chef was *cool*), but far too often in my experience, my "expert" advice was requested and then promptly ignored or questioned. I was often asked about meat temperatures and always got the same response. After I gave the meat a feel with my finger and pronounced it to be medium rare, the cook (a friend or family member) would look at me and say *No . . . let's give it a few more minutes.* More than once, I'd tried to correct a friend's knife skills for his or her own safety: *Put the flat side down,* I would offer; *there'll be less chance of it slipping and you cutting yourself.* But most people really just want to continue doing things their own way. So, unless my help was expressly requested, I stayed out of other people's kitchens and drank my glass of wine far from any dinner preparations, which was fine with me. I was (and remain) happy to relax and be a guest, no matter how imperfectly prepared the meal.

But simply being a guest at a dinner party isn't always without its pitfalls. People often likened me to the "chefs" they saw on TV, many of whom I unfortunately had never heard of. Like most chefs, I had little time and even less inclination to watch food television; my life *was* food television, only faster, meaner, and lower paid. In fact, most chefs express pure disgust for the likes of the permanently perky Rachael Ray, with her emphatic and recurring admission that she's no chef. Lots of chefs and cooks blame user-friendly TV chefs along with food-themed kids' movies like *Ratatouille* for sugar-coating the harsh realities of working in a kitchen. *Oh, no,* they worry when a cute movie like *Ratatouille* comes out, *now every sniveling kid is going to want to be a chef.* Top Chef was a welcome addition and antidote to the previous glut of unrealistic food programming. Finally, cooks had a show that not only represented their world but respected and rewarded it. Suddenly everyone was watching *Top Chef* (not just restaurant people), and cooking, *real* cooking, was in the spotlight.

So, when Matt asked for my help with a party where I'd be not only a guest but also a cohost, I set one ground rule: He had to listen to me and follow directions; my reputation as a professional was on the line! And he did. When I corrected the way he cut an onion for the truffled mushroom risotto, he quietly did it my way without complaining. And he didn't whine when I gently chided him to keep stirring the risotto after adding some chicken stock or when I urged him to add more salt when seasoning the roast chicken. He was amazed that we never measured anything, even the ingredients for the caramel sauce and pecan brittle we made for the sundaes. Over the years, I explained, some measurements just become ingrained in your head and you get a feel for things.

If only I held as much sway in my job at Tonic. A year later, the food remained as good as always, but despite the restaurant's many accolades, business had begun to slow, and once again we found ourselves trying to unravel the mysterious equation that results in a successful restaurant. It was frustrating for everyone, not least of all the owner. As an owner of several restaurants, he should have been accustomed to the finicky ups and downs of the business; nevertheless he got into the habit of loitering in my dessert station during the afternoon hours. Both hands in his front pockets, he would rock forward on his toes and then back onto his heels, shaking his head: *Oh, we are losing money. . . . Business is not good. . . . What am I going to do?* He just stood around, talking to the air or venting his thoughts to me, I never knew which.

The writing was soon on the wall, and we began hearing rumors (the restaurant world is a small one) that Uncle Steve, as we called the owner, was preparing to sell part of the business to a new chef. It was only a matter of time—weeks, maybe—before we would once again be leaving a restaurant that had not lived up to our expectations for any length of time.

✥

TWENTY-THREE

Rolling with the Punches

For almost two years after leaving Tonic, I floated from consulting job to consulting job, helping out chefs in small restaurants who had neither the time nor the space to support a full-time pastry chef. Most chefs are too preoccupied with opening or running their restaurants to worry about coming up with desserts, and I discovered that my ability to relieve them of this worry was a great commodity. These restaurants needed simple but pleasing desserts that fit their food style and that their staffs could execute when I was no longer there. The money for these jobs was usually pretty good, and I had much more control over my own schedule: I could commit to a few weeks or a few months. After working with Joey for so many years, a tiny part of me worried about achieving success out from under his protective wing, but consulting for new chefs proved that I did not need Joey, that my talents were all my own. Consulting also introduced me to new chefs, new ideas, and totally new food styles, some of which were completely at odds with everything I'd grown used to.

I connected with Barton, an African-American chef who was opening a small West Village restaurant, because we had worked for the same restaurant group years earlier and knew a lot of the same people. My interview with him was casual, but it was clear he was totally committed to his career. I knew next to nothing about his food style, which he described as "American as influenced by the African Diaspora," but I was fascinated by his seemingly endless knowledge of all kinds of food. Not only did he casually throw around words like *calas, bolo de apim,* and *philpy,* but he gave me their detailed definition as well as their anthropological background and the route through which they derived. He was a species I had not yet encountered in restaurant kitchens: the intellectual. It seemed he had vast stores of information about everything from jazz to art to history, and he was like a mad scientist in the kitchen, throwing what seemed to me way too many ingredients into a pot, taking too many steps, and combining too many ethnicities only to succeed in creating an amazing new flavor or dish. I'd gotten used to the simple elegance of French techniques and Mediterranean flavors, but Barton opened up a whole new way of approaching food. With the help of everything he taught me, I developed a recipe for *calas,* New Orleans fritters, using leftover rice, and a sweet potato crème caramel that was served with a lime gelée. Barton had suggested the unusual flavor combination, and, to my surprise, it totally worked. I was reminded that cooking and food provide endless opportunities to learn and grow. When my time at Barton's restaurant was over, we remained friends, brought together by a love of food and an eagerness to learn new things.

In those years, Joey finally opened his very own restaurant in the West Village, Extra Virgin, which became an instant success. It was the place he had always dreamed of opening: an unpretentious neighborhood restaurant where the food is interesting, well executed, and delicious. He had neither the space nor the need for a pastry chef, but I did everything I could to make sure his desserts were easy to execute and delicious. Once we had the desserts set up, Joey no longer needed my assistance, and I knew that our eight-year work partnership had come to an end.

After two years of consulting, I was ready, once again, for some routine—at the very least, health insurance. But as much as I wanted the stability of a full-time job and the prestige of working in a restaurant of high repute, I had trepidations about returning to a six-day, sixty-plus-hour work week. I was older, and my life fuller. I was no longer interested in having a monogamous relationship with work. It was a dilemma, but before I could even start exploring my options, Barton called to tell me about a job he'd heard about, one he thought would be perfect. *The hours are great,* Barton told me, knowing my ambivalence about returning to a full-time restaurant job. *You'll have time for other things in your life.* He claimed it was a pastry chef job with "bankers' hours" at a three-star restaurant. This was unheard of. When Joey called a few days later urging me to look into the very same job, I had to take notice.

I sat across from the chef in the small basement office of Veritas. He leaned back in the office chair, relaxed, and slumped, his legs spread wide, his hair flopped forward over his face. His chef's pants were rolled up well above his ankles. The office was crowded with stacks of boxes, endless bits of paper were stuck to the walls, and the drop ceiling was missing most of its tiles.

"So," he said, in a thick Boston accent, "we're a very civilized restaurant. The pastry chef *wahks* five days. For the most *pahht,* I'm very easy to get along with. There's not a lot of yelling . . . as long as no one fucks with my service. I can't have my service fucked with."

"Right," I said, nodding.

"I like simple desserts," he went on. "Simple. A lemon tart. None of this architectural crap. Simple. The garde-manger guy has to be able to plate them at night so the plates can't be too complicated."

"Okay," I said. He just looked at me. I'd never been good at interviews, at being put on the spot. I wished he would ask me something. He didn't.

"Do you want to see my book?" I offered. I held out the large black portfolio I'd been building over the years. It held most of the press I had received, and had plenty of pictures. It was proof to both of us that I was, in fact, a real pastry chef.

"My stuff is pretty simple," I said as he took the book and started flipping through it. "I like clean lines, more of a Scandinavian or Asian aesthetic. I really like things to taste good and look appealing. But definitely they have to taste good." He handed the book back to me.

"The thing is," he explained, "that if you take the job, I'd want you to commit to at least a year, because finding a pastry chef is a pain in the ass."

I nodded.

"So, why don't you think about it. Call me the day after tomorrow."

I left the restaurant, my mind already dizzy. A three-star restaurant, dinner only, and a five-day work week? And it was a prix-fixe restaurant so I wouldn't even have to worry about how many customers ordered dessert because *every* customer got dessert. With only fifty seats, the dining room was small, and the salary was decent. The chef seemed nice enough, not condescending or arrogant as a lot of chefs can be. The kitchen had a reputation for being nice, with cooks that stayed on for years—a sure sign of a good work environment. And I wasn't even asked to do a tasting. The job had practically fallen into my lap.

"Well," the chef said when I called back two days later, "the job's *yahs* if you want it."

I hadn't asked him about health insurance or vacation or any of the other things I was supposed to ask a potential employer at that stage of my career. I simply reacted, as I had so many times in the past, based on gut feeling.

Three weeks later, I started working at Veritas. I knew it would take some time to change the six-item dessert menu, but I was determined to do a special on my very first day. I decided on a dessert I'd done before with much success: a lemon tart, something the chef had mentioned during my interview. Why not let him know I was willing to take his suggestions to heart? Too many pastry chefs tried too hard to establish their independence, but I was used to a collaborative relationship with Joey. I wanted to make my chef happy.

I pressed a dark brown sugar crust into the bottom of a shallow ring mold and baked it. When it cooled, I filled the ring to the top with lemon curd that had just the barest amount of gelatin added to keep it molded. Once the curd set up in the fridge, I unmolded the tarts by heating the outside of the metal ring mold with a propane torch, warming the curd just enough to allow the ring mold to be smoothly lifted off. Then, I piped thick spikes of Italian meringue (egg whites and sugar cooked to 240 degrees Fahrenheit) to conceal the entire top of the tart. Just before the dessert went out to a table, the meringue would get "torched," gently toasted with the propane torch so that it looked, and tasted, like a toasted marshmallow. Joey had always referred to the dessert as the Don King because of its spiky top. I had just finished the crusts when Felix, my new assistant, who came with the job, arrived at work.

"Hi," he said. He was pale, with thick, dark hair. He seemed like the kind of guy who had a permanent five o'clock shadow. He had a thick Slavic accent and smelled like cigarettes and after-shave. "So, I need the last Sunday of the month off."

It was bad enough that he had arrived fifteen minutes late, but now he was telling me that he needed one of *my* days off. In the restaurant business, Sunday is *the* day off, the best day, and the day that nearly every chef and pastry chef takes as his or her own. I was no exception, and I had every intention of maintaining my schedule. I just looked at him.

"You don't have to give it to me," he explained, "but my

friends are taking me out drinking for my birthday the night before, so I'm just telling you that I am not going to be in on that Sunday."

Though he had graduated recently from a local pastry arts program and had been at Veritas for almost a year, he didn't have much of a reputation. Chef had given me permission to get rid of him if I wanted, even saying that he wasn't the sharpest tool in the box. He hadn't said anything about him being a jerk.

"Let me just look at my calendar," I told him coldly. "I don't think it'll be a problem."

As much as I wanted to deny his absurd sense of entitlement, set a precedent, and show him who was boss, I decided to bide my time. He'd made a terrible first impression, but I didn't want to make too rash a decision. It could take weeks to find a decent assistant, and in the meantime I would be left to do all of his work *and* mine, and I wouldn't have any days off. I left Felix setting up the station in the upstairs kitchen, which had all the stoves and ovens, and went downstairs to finish my special, already imagining how I'd phrase my Craigslist ad for a new assistant.

At Veritas, the chef gave me only a few guidelines to work with. Aside from wanting the desserts to be kept simple, he also disliked anything that sounded too "homey" or American. So, I could make my golden pineapple upside down cake, but I had to call it "golden pineapple financier," which sounded perfectly reasonable to me. He had only two requirements: that I make some sort of cake batter that could be piped into small madeleine molds, baked to order, and used as petits fours, and that the chocolate soufflé remain on the menu. It was Veritas's top-selling dessert, and the recipe had remained unchanged since their opening seven years earlier.

The chocolate soufflé was not a soufflé at all but a variation of chocolate molten cake. It was the one dessert I had avoided my entire career, the dessert I had for so long despised, if only for its sheer omnipresence and lack of imagination. But after nine years of detesting it, I came to appreciate its one undeniable strength: People loved it. It was warm and oozing and chocolate, and it was served with ice cream. With the mandated chocolate soufflé on my menu, there was no pressure to come up with a rich, chocolate dessert, the one that had always been trickiest for me. Knowing that customers wouldn't be denied their gooey-chocolate desires, I was free to make less intense chocolate desserts, cool chocolate desserts, chocolate desserts with more interesting flavor combinations.

Slowly I phased in all my new desserts. Some, like a pumpkin crème caramel with coconut cream and rum raisins, were very successful. The customers loved it, as did the cooks and waiters, who were happy to gobble down any leftovers. Others, though, like the lemon tart, which I had added to the menu, did not go over as well. I was devastated when the chef suggested I change my tart because it "looked too similar" to another dessert (they were made in the same mold).

Thankfully it was the first and only time that any of my desserts got knocked down by the chef. Over time, I figured out what kinds of desserts worked, what matched the food: French-inspired but with some license taken and, for the most part, quite rich. Veritas has one of the best wine lists in the country, and so the food, as well as the desserts, had to complement the wine. I took my lead from the savory food: I toned down the whimsy of my desserts and kept my plates simple, I used mostly seasonal ingredients, and most important, I kept my flavors delicious and unfussy. As I grew more confident, I began adding less obvious, more adventurous flavors: white pepper ice cream, for example, with an apple-rhubarb crisp, saffron cream with a coconut panna cotta, Thai coffee ice cream with the chocolate soufflé. I wanted diners to be happily surprised to discover the unfamiliar flavor.

Since Veritas had received three stars from the *New York Times* years earlier and had long since gotten rid of their public relations company, I didn't have to worry about impending reviews, and I'd gotten far enough along in my own career that I no longer yearned for press the way I once had. I was happy just being a pastry chef in a stellar restaurant with steady business. But other challenges lay ahead of me, and Felix was just the beginning.

✤

TWENTY-FOUR

Fruits and Nuts

Dalia!" bellowed the voice as Culo, robust as usual, walked into the kitchen.

"Hi, Culo," I answered.

It took me a while to get used to calling him Culo, which means "ass" in Spanish. When I first started, Culo was on a two-month leave of absence due to a broken arm. Before his return, he'd come up in conversation among the cooks all the time, and when I asked why they called him Culo, the answer was always "You'll see." Later, I figured it was a nickname he'd earned from the other guys in the kitchen on account of his loud mouth, and the stupid things that came out of it. It wasn't until I saw his given name—Justin Couleau—printed out on a paycheck envelope that I discovered he didn't need a nickname. That it was spelled differently made no difference. Everyone heard "Culo."

Culo's arrival each day signified the end of my quiet morning. For two days each week, my assistant, The Albanian (who didn't seem to mind the name the other cooks had given him), was blessedly off, and I had the kitchen all to myself. I'd been too preoccupied with getting acclimated to Veritas to focus on finding a new assistant, so I had to tolerate The Albanian's inane stories about his loose connections to the Albanian mafia, his wedding preparations, his plans to sell real estate because pastry wasn't "really what he wanted to do." I was actually overjoyed when he told me he needed to leave early three days a week for a real estate class.

Soon the rest of the cooks would arrive, and the kitchen, which had been all mine since eight that morning, would be overrun with boys. They were, for the most part, all nice guys and good cooks, but they were boys nonetheless, despite being in their twenties. They took over the kitchen, bringing with them meat and garlic, sloshing stocks, and spattering hot oil, along with the annoying cacophony of the classic rock station and their even louder mouths. It was no place for a pastry chef like me, whose work depended on exacting methods, straight lines, and careful measurements. I preferred my work environment to be calm and orderly, with the gentle voices of the local public radio station in the background. I switched off the radio and retreated to my pastry area in the basement, where I spent the balance of my day.

My station in the basement was modest: a six-foot stainless steel table, a fourth of which was occupied by an ice cream machine. The ice creams at Veritas were spun every day, so they were always soft and creamy and could be quenelled, or scooped, using only spoons. I also had my own set of shelves on which to store pastry ingredients, and half of the dairy walk-in. Most pastry chefs are anal retentive about their areas and tools, and I was no exception. But we have good reason: Plenty of cooks thoughtlessly use and misplace pastry tools, move pastry *mise-en-place* to make room for their own, and simply regard pastry as less important. I was happy to find that no one at Veritas really messed with the pastry area or *mise-en-place.* Maybe it was because every new cook at Veritas had to master garde-manger before moving up, which meant mastering the dessert plates, too. It was something they all had to get past, and respect, before moving on to what they considered "real" cooking.

"Hey, Miyagi!" Culo yelled.

Miyagi, né Carlos, was the butcher/prep guy with whom I shared the basement area. His prep table was just across from mine. He had been dubbed Miyagi because of the slow and steady way in which he worked, just like the sensei in *The Karate Kid.* Nicknames abounded in almost every restaurant I'd ever worked in, but Veritas, arguably the most prestigious restaurant on my résumé, turned out to be an absolute treasure trove of name-calling. One cook was Cabezón, on account of his big head, and the award-winning wine director who sported longish, strawberry-blond hair was called Peluca, or "wig." No one was immune to the name game. Even the chef took full ownership of his nickname, Chatos, which means "small nosed" in Spanish. It was the equivalent of calling a bald person Curly.

"Did Truffle Boy come today?" Culo asked Miyagi.

Truffle Boy was the guy who delivered truffle oil, truffle butter, and, when in season, the incredibly expensive whole, fresh
truffles. His family owned the small French truffle company for
which he worked, and though he was a man in his late twenties, I
never heard him called anything other than Truffle Boy, or simply Truf. On occasion his name became All Balls and No Cock,
but that's another story.

"No," answered Miyagi. He also received all the deliveries.
"No truffles coming today."

"What about pussy?" asked Culo, grinning. "We get any pussy
in today?"

"No, not yet," answered Miyagi calmly. "Octopus coming
later."

It still amazed me, even after so many years, that the moment
male cooks walk through the kitchen doors into the "back of the
house," their inner ten-year-olds are suddenly unleashed and with
it a glee for saying dirty words (in public! to girls!). They took
every opportunity to replace common words with more profane
ones: *Striped bass,* for example, routinely became *striped ass.*

The kitchen was full of boys, and their majority ruled. Some
women working in kitchens decide to join them (since there is little chance of beating them) and try to match them vulgarity for
vulgarity, sexual comment (or conquest) for sexual comment. But
consistent indifference was my preferred tactic. I'd gotten pretty
good at ignoring a lot of the dirty talk, let alone the porn that often popped up on the computer when I started work in the morning (a sure sign that the night before had been slow) and the endless
array of "business" cards advertising phone numbers of mostly

naked women. A collage of these cards on the inside door of a lowboy refrigerator surprised a female health inspector one morning, though she made no mention of it in her report. The kitchen favorite featured a scantily clad woman suggestively holding an ear of shucked corn. For months, the cooks endlessly asked each other and everyone else, *Do you like corn? Te gustas maiz?* Even when I thought the cooks were funny, and the bizarre voice and face that accompanied the corn question was undeniably funny, I tried not to let it show. I was not always successful.

"What are you working on, Dalia?" Culo asked, walking past me again.

"Passion fruit cheesecake," I told him. "I'm adding it to the menu tonight."

Though I vehemently disagreed with most of what Culo did and said as sous-chef, he was in a position of authority, so I tried to be as civil as possible. I usually finished work before dinner service, which meant my desserts were in the hands of the cooks. I wanted Culo to watch out for my stuff when I wasn't there.

"Sounds good," he said, and walked away.

"Beanbag!" The yell traveled from the kitchen, down the stairs, to my ears.

Beanbag didn't even work there anymore, but his nickname became so popular that it garnered a cult following and often could be heard echoing spontaneously through the building. "Beanbag!" while searching for a bottle of Chianti wine vinegar. "Beanbag!" while slicing the cured salmon. "Beanbag!" upon entering the kitchen. Every day. Likewise, The Angry Jew, a former curmudgeonly cook who had scowled at every special request, lived on through the cooks' imitations of him. *What? You want me to put a candle on the dessert? Maybe I should just go out there and sing happy fucking birthday, too. What is this, T.G.I. Friday's?*

"Beanbag!"

Everything I needed for my new dessert was ready. With the cheesecakes still in their rings, I used a small offset spatula to coat each one with a thin, even layer of passion fruit curd. Then I un-molded them by heating each ring with a propane torch while spinning it on a rotating cake table. I gathered the rest of the gar-nish for the desserts: wine-stewed berries and Sicilian pistachios. For the berries I had reduced some red wine by almost three quar-ters with cinnamon stick, bay leaf, and vanilla bean, then poured the hot reduction over blueberries and blackberries. I added the raspberries once the others were cooled so they wouldn't break down and turn to unattractive mush. The cheesecakes had regular pistachios in the crust, but I used the expensive, jewel-like Sicilian pistachios as a garnish: three nuts on the top of each cheesecake. As I did with every new or special dessert, I would introduce the passion fruit cheesecake to the waiters while they ate family meal, so they would know firsthand what they were serving.

"That's how *Rawd* likes it!"

Chatos turned out to be the biggest kid of all, especially when it came to nicknames and random outbursts. Chatos's "Beanbags" were always the loudest and the most forceful: He used his entire body to yell, stopping in his tracks to bellow with a full body arch. And though he loved "Beanbag," he also liked to yell about some impending fictional "anal jihad," though to what, exactly, he was referring I never really knew. *Anal jihad is coming, my friend!* he would yell in a voice that sounded a little bit like Yoda on crack. *Abdullah is gonna get you! Face the east and take it from the west!*

"Come on!" yelled one of the cooks, in a faux British accent, responding to Chatos. "That's it!"

Meredith, a waiter, should have known better than to tell them about the night she met Rod Stewart on the street and ended up having drinks with him late into the night. Just drinks, though, she swore, at a bar. And even though he'd actually sung to her that night and left a message on her cell phone (she said), she never heard from him again. The guys had been using her story as ammunition in an incessant barrage of teasing ever since.

"Come on!" I heard again. "Lick me balls. Tickle 'em!"

It had to be close to four o'clock, time for family meal. I brought my cheesecakes to the walk-in and went upstairs to the kitchen. Sure enough, Meredith, plate in hand, was waiting in line for her serving of Linguine Prima Leftover: linguine with a hodgepodge of inexpensive vegetables in a buttery cream sauce that might or might not have contained cheese. I got in line, right under a picture of Rod Stewart that someone had kindly torn from a magazine and taped onto the "wall of fame," right next to a wine label from a 1962 Châteauneuf-du-Pape, a few photos of Chatos at an event with another well-known chef, and two photos of the legendary six-fingered dishwasher, in one of which he is waving.

"C'mon, Meredith," said Culo in his regular voice, stepping past her. "Tell us how Rod likes it."

"You guys," she said, smiling in mock anger. It was her only comeback, and it was a futile one. She just kept shaking her head as she moved along in the small line until she stood in front of the bowl of pasta and the bain-marie of *agua fresca* (family punch) I'd made with leftover passion fruit puree.

"What's this?" she said, lifting the ladle in and out of the punch over and over.

"Nipple punch," answered Carter, a young cook, standing across from her.

"Huh?" she said, still idly emptying ladle after ladle back into the bain-marie.

"Nipple punch," Carter said again, not missing a beat, staring right at her, deadpan.

I then noticed what she was wearing: a flesh-colored, sheer, clingy shirt, through which her nipples did indeed show. She still didn't get the joke, and Carter didn't let her in on it. She just took her bowl of pasta and went out to the dining room to eat with the rest of the waiters.

I ate my bowl of pasta standing in the kitchen with the rest of the cooks and then double-checked all the desserts and respective garnishes and sauces on the dessert station. It was the perfect time for this, since the boys usually settled down a bit during family meal, enjoying the lull before the storm of dinner service. As I went through all the *mise-en-place,* I kept a mental list of everything that needed to be replenished or freshened: caramel sauce, sliced Medjool dates, roasted cocoa beans . . .

"Hey, Dalia," said Carter, interrupting my train of thought. I pulled my head out of the lowboy and looked up from my squat.

"Yeah?"

"Did you know," he continued, "that the band Steely Dan got its name from a dildo in the movie *Naked Lunch*?"

The rest of the guys kept their heads down, pretending not to listen. I stood up.

"Carter," I told him in the same bored tone I'd use to explain the difference between Italian and Swiss meringues, "Steely Dan was around before that movie came out."

"Rats," he said under his breath, shaking his fist. He turned back to his cutting board.

Carter may or may not have realized that *Naked Lunch* was a book long before it became a movie, but I didn't want to get drawn any further into a conversation about dildos, which was what I was pretty sure he was hoping for. Consistent indifference, I told myself going downstairs. Consistent indifference.

I hastily brought up all the components of my new dessert and showed Labios how to plate the cheesecake. *They call me Labios,* he had told me, *on account of my big crazy lips.* He did indeed have insanely full lips, along with an incredibly good nature and sharp wit, in both English and Spanish. Labios was quickly becoming one of my favorite people in the restaurant (his *te gustas maiz* was the most hilarious), though I tried not to let it show. Aside from Chatos, he was the only person I really trusted with my desserts. Thankfully, he worked garde-manger nearly every night.

I brought my new dessert out to the waiters, who ate their family meal at a large round table in the dining room. After setting the plate on the table, I stood there, waiting for them to quiet down. In every restaurant it's the same thing. Before I can start my explanation, they start guessing.

"What's that?"

"Is it a lemon tart?"

"I know! Mango!"

Rather than talk over them, I simply stood there waiting for them, all of them, to quiet down, so I could say my piece. It was a tactic that worked quite well, though it always made me feel more like a kindergarten teacher than a pastry chef. I announced the dessert as it would appear on the menu: Pistachio-Crusted Passion Fruit Cheesecake with Wine-Stewed Berries. I went over each component, trying not to roll my eyes when someone asked if it had nuts. Waiters have an inordinate amount of power when it comes to suggesting dishes, since diners invariably ask them what they like best on the menu. I wanted them to try my new dessert, love it, and suggest it.

After family meal, I finished up the rest of my work downstairs and made a list of things to be ordered for the next day as well as a to-do list. I then headed back to the dingy unisex locker room to change into my civilian clothing. Cooks and waiters shared the same small room, filthy from constantly flooding sewer water and the bags of dirty, fermenting linen. Filth is an inevitable fact of restaurant life. Even Joey, obsessive about cleanliness and order, could not stop the kitchen floor drains from overflowing and sometimes spewing sewage. Visitors to kitchens are usually appalled by the grimy floors (grimy even though they're mopped twice a day), the crumbling walls, and greasy exhaust hoods—the filth that cooks deal with every day. But diners shouldn't worry.

In any good restaurant, food is always stored and handled with the utmost care, even if cooks have to walk through two inches of dirty water to get to it.

I stood on my dirty chef's coat while changing. Just as I was finishing, Meredith came in and smiled as she slumped into the single chair in the room, her short-shorts riding up.

"Dalia," she said thoughtfully, smiling. "Your titties must be filled with milk chocolate."

"Huh?" I said, trying to get past her to give her more room.

"Because everything you make tastes so good," she explained innocently.

"Thanks," I mumbled, grabbing my bag and heading out the door.

I made my way down the dimly lit hallway that led back to the basement, carefully balancing on the slabs of wood that someone had kindly laid down in the puddles of leftover floodwater. I made a mental note to be careful about wearing sandals in the warmer months. The usually treacherous hallway was the only route back to the basement and out of the restaurant.

"You outta here?" asked Chatos, seeing me in my street clothes. I nodded, as I took one last look at my list of things to be ordered for the next day.

Chatos was settled at his spot in front of a cutting board a few feet away from my pastry station. He was still working on finishing up the butchering that the prep guy had started earlier that day. He made all the final cuts on the meat, fish, and foie gras, rendering the cleaned slabs of flesh into expertly sculpted and perfectly portioned shapes.

"You know Culo's gay, right?" he asked.

Culo, I had already gathered, was many things—a chauvinist, hypocrite, loudmouth, misogynist, homophobe, borderline bigot—but as far as I could tell, he was definitely not gay.

"Get out!" I answered dryly, turning to him with faux wide eyes. I was still trying to figure out how to respond to my new chef's outrageous behavior. I turned back to my list, adding a box of 61 percent chocolate pistols.

"GAY!" yelled Chatos at the top of his lungs, bending his knees and throwing back his head. "GAAAAAAAY!!!"

Chatos had started the teasing months earlier, and what started out as good-natured ribbing against a self-proclaimed "man of hate" had snowballed into a new animal all its own, one that was as gargantuan in its size as it was merciless in its execution.

"He likes it in the AAAAAAY!" Chatos added, screaming.

Pause.

"Twice on Sun-DAY!" came another burst, to no one in particular. Chatos's outbursts were so free and forceful, so persistent, that I became convinced he suffered from both autism and Tourette's. Most restaurants exist within an atmosphere that encourages constant insults, teasing, and general adolescent ribbing, but the "Culo is gay" phenomenon was far beyond anything I could have imagined. Chatos had made a conscious and absolute decision to run the "Culo is gay" gag every day. Common sense or common management guidelines might dictate that the boss should be the last one encouraging the rest of the employees to tease and disrespect his sous-chef—his second in command, of all people—

but I was quickly learning that common sense did not apply to Veritas kitchen politics.

"Chatos," said Stewart, suddenly sticking his head out from the sommelier office. Stewart could hear everything from in there. He looked down the hallway, making sure the coast was clear.

"Dude, maybe you should chill out with the gay stuff," he said, smiling. He didn't sound very convincing. "Culo got really pissed last night."

Stewart explained how, the night before, he went online and found a rhyming website. He spent the rest of the night sharing the wealth with the kitchen, reciting a never-ending ode to Culo: *Culo is gay . . . he likes it in the AY . . . from a guy named Andre . . . when he's in Taipei . . . with boys he likes to roll in the hay . . . even if he has to pay.*

"Poor Culo," Chatos said, shaking his head. He paused before confidently raising his head and smiling. "Fuck Culo!" he yelled valiantly.

He paused again, thinking. "Nah," he decided. "I don't wanna fuck Culo. He's too ugly. Maybe just his lips. That's it."

Stewart laughed, shaking his head.

It would have been easy to write Chatos off as simply irritating, or immature, or even sadistic (and he did take occasional pride in calling himself a sadist), except that his cooks loved him. He was outrageous and funny and smart, and they not only looked up to him, they worshipped him. Their eyes would light up with delight at every bizarrely inappropriate word that came out of his mouth. That he was superlatively talented and generous with his knowledge only meant they loved him more. I would have found him impossible to tolerate if he weren't, as strange as it sounds, fair and not the slightest bit arrogant. We had very few serious conversations about my work, but when we did, he was always surprisingly professional. I actually liked him.

"Dude," Chatos said when Culo finally ventured into the basement. "When are you gonna come out of the closet?"

"I'm *not* gay," Culo insisted. He was sick of the gay jokes, but Chatos, his chef, was the one and only person in the restaurant he could not tell to fuck off. He was helpless and had to take the abuse. All of it. Every day. The rest of us certainly didn't mind.

"Dude," Chatos countered, "you watch *American Idol.* You probably watch it in bed with a big bottle of Jergens lotion and a box of Kleenex."

It was his most stalwart evidence. Who else but a gay guy watches *American Idol*? Culo also made the mistake of admitting he'd gone by himself to see *Miami Vice* in the movie theater. *That's fucking gay. It doesn't get any gayer than that.* Culo became a new benchmark for gay. If Styx, for example, was broadcast on the radio, Chatos instantly changed the station. *Oh God, that song isn't just gay; it's Culo gay.* The only thing Chatos hated more than gay music was a Rachael Ray commercial. *Oh, kill me now,* he would say upon hearing her cheery voice on the radio.

Shaking my head, I stepped into the small office to place my order, hoping that Chatos's yells were not audible on the other end of the line. Finally, I made my way out of the basement, irritated that I could not stop myself from thinking of more words that rhyme with *gay*. On the stairs, I ran into Culo, who was still shaking his head at Chatos.

"Geez," Culo said to me, eyes wide. "I don't know what to do. I think he really thinks I'm gay!"

Despite his tendency to be asinine, disrespectful, and insulting, I liked to believe that Culo's loudmouthing was as much an act as Chatos's, that it was just posturing and that underneath it all, he was a decent guy. I liked to think that, but it didn't make him any more likable or trustworthy. I knew he was venting to me only as a last resort; everyone else in the restaurant was in on the gag.

"It's driving me crazy, Dalia!" he said.

"You know," I offered, "it's not about you. It's got nothing to do with whether or not you're gay," I told him. After all the months of torment, he still hadn't figured out what most of us figured out in second grade and what the cooks so clearly took advantage of: The more he protested and showed his upset, the more fun it was to continue the abuse.

✦

TWENTY-FIVE

After Hours

I walked into work one morning and found the bar littered with dirty wineglasses, empty bottles, and cigarette ashes. Had it not been for the broken glass on the floor, the wine stain on the wall, and the two upended tables, it might have been like any other day. I took off my jacket, hung it in the coat check, and grabbed some coffee before going to check out the dining room. An entire section of the normally neatly arranged room was completely disheveled—tablecloths bundled on the floor, place settings out of order, and tables at cockeyed angles. One of the upended tables was actually broken, its top partially separated from its pedestal.

"I know," said my new assistant, Peter, suddenly emerging from the kitchen, coffee cup in hand. Cooks drink enormous amounts of coffee.

Peter showed up at the restaurant one morning not too long after I started at Veritas. He'd staged (worked for free) for the previous pastry chef one day a week and asked to continue to stage with me, and he'd arrived just in time. I'd just about had it with The Albanian who, in addition to being generally inadequate, took too many cigarette breaks, talked on his cell phone in the kitchen (Cell phone in the kitchen? Was he kidding?), and had a nasty tendency to make blatantly racist and sexist remarks. Just when he had pushed me over the edge, Peter appeared and accepted my offer to be my full-time assistant. Not only was Peter more than adequate as an assistant, but he was familiar with the kitchen and the cooks, too. Maybe too familiar. The cooks called him Stinky Peter because of what they perceived to be a body odor problem.

"This is fucked up, right?" Peter said.

"Yeah." I nodded, taking it all in. "It was like this when you got here?"

"Uh-huh," he answered.

"Nobody else is here?" It was not unusual to arrive in the morning and find someone passed out on table seventeen's banquette.

"Nope," he replied. "Just me and David." David was the new prep guy.

"Huh."

"And get a load of this!" he said proudly.

Peter directed me back to the floor at the end of the bar and pointed down to a clump of hair. A clump of actual human hair!

"Check it out." He crouched down closer, pointing purposefully to the dark brown thatch. "It's got highlights," he said triumphantly. "It's gotta be from Chatos. He's the only one with highlights."

He was right. Chatos was the only one with highlights. It was weird enough that he *had* highlights, let alone that they'd been pulled out and left on the floor. We walked back to the broken table in search of more clues.

"Holy crap!" Peter said, getting a closer look. "Is that blood? Or wine?"

I peered at the reddish brown drops on a neighboring tablecloth and shrugged.

"Who knows?" I answered nonchalantly.

Leaving the scene undisturbed, we walked back to the kitchen. Peter got back to work setting up the dessert station for the night's service, and I went downstairs to change into my chef's jacket and clogs.

I'd like to say that finding the restaurant in such a state was a shock, but it wasn't. The extent of the damage was unusual but not completely outside the realm of possibility. All kinds of stuff happens in restaurants at night after the customers are gone, the work is done, and the unwinding (i.e., drinking) begins, and Veritas was no exception. I could assess the previous night's debauchery by how much urine (or vomit or excrement) was left on the women's toilet seat.

Most independently run restaurants have alter egos, suppressed (usually alcoholic) personalities whose liberation each night coincides with closing time. As the last customers take their seats in the dining room and their orders print out in the kitchen, someone is already putting the beer on ice. Sometimes a particular brand of beer is ordered for the sole purpose of satisfying the thirst of the cooks. Sometimes it's a cheap variety, but just as often it's a quality import because, well, cooks work hard, earn little money, and deserve a decent beer at the end of the night. When it becomes clear that all the orders are in, the cooks begin to close down their stations. Once the crunch is over and there are no more unknowns, it's time to relax. Time for a beer. It's beer o'clock.

One of the first things I learned as a young cook was how to open a bottle of beer without a bottle opener. The hinge end of a pair of tongs works very nicely, ditto wedging the cap between the metal slats of a metro shelf. I was less proficient with the edge of a counter or the butt end of a chef's knife but still never had any problems consuming my nightly reward for a job well done. Cold beer does go down easy after four or five sweltering hours of hellish service.

And so every night, cooks, with their abundant reward of free alcohol, relax after a day's work, just like lots of regular people relax with a drink after work. The difference is that happy hour for cooks begins at midnight, lasts longer than an hour, and is largely funded and encouraged by their employers. And even when these employers have the good sense to limit the drinks, it does little to hamper the overall intake because when you work six nights a week until at least eleven p.m., if you want to have any semblance of a social life, you must have it at night. And what is available to a young cook or waiter at this late hour? Bars. Every restaurant crew has a local bar they frequent. Every one. And who else is awake and interested in socializing at this late hour? Other cooks and waiters, who are in exactly the same boat. The very same waiters the cooks bitch about all night become cohorts once service is over and the drinks begin to work their lubricious magic. The combination of (mostly) young men and women, large amounts of alcohol, the hours of midnight through dawn, and stressful work results in antics that are more reminiscent of a frat house than of a fine dining establishment and usually end in one of three ways: the hookup, the solitary pass out, the fight.

As with the stereotypical frat boy, a cook's need for conquest is ever-present, and thus the amount of interrestaurant relations is astounding. And because cooks make little effort to keep their exploits to themselves, I know much, much more than I really care to. *Her tits hang down to, like, here, Doll,* a cook told me, slicing his hand across his belly. *And Alex? She's a maniac! An animal in the sack!* another said one day, eyebrows raised in exaggeration. Maybe they were trying to impress me, but more likely, I think, I was just another cook, even if I was a woman, a pastry chef, and their senior. I worked side by side with them in the kitchen and was therefore privy to their sexploits and certainly not protected from them. *Have you seen how hairy her arms are?* a cook rhetorically asked me. *You can imagine the rest of her. . . .* What I couldn't imagine is why these young girls so easily fell victim to these loose-lipped cooks. How did so many of the cute waiters find themselves in bed with these pasty-faced, spongy-looking dogs with the stink of oil and food still under their fingernails and in their hair? It's amazing how a couple of hours and a few drinks can bring people together.

All of this is not to say that I have not indulged in the occasional late-night sexploit. I've had my share of waiter one-night stands, drunken coworker sleepovers, and chef affairs. I briefly made out with my debonair sixty-year-old French chef and once took part in an after work game of all-female-coworker spin the bottle—and that was before kissing girls became fashionable. I am in no position to judge.

For every late night that results in a coupling, there is an equal number that end with the solitude of the severe hangover. I came in one morning and found Carter, a cook, asleep on a banquette in the darkest corner of the dining room. *NO! No lights,* he moaned painfully as I slid the dimmer switches up. *Please . . . no lights.* He'd startled me but not half as much as he'd startled the new young prep guy, David, who came to work at seven a.m. that morning and found him locked *into* the restaurant, left behind when the last of the nighttime dishwashers had locked up for the evening.

David found Carter passed out in the customer bathroom, head resting on the toilet seat and pants pulled down around his ankles, toilet still not flushed from the night before. Not a pretty picture. Luckily for Carter and me both, David pulled up Carter's pants, flushed the toilet, dragged him over to a banquette, and tucked him under a chef's jacket. When it came time for Carter to set up his station and work, everyone sympathized with his green, puffy, silent face, allowing him ample space to sweat it out as well as time to retreat to the staff bathroom to puke. It wasn't the first time someone had spent a drunken night on the banquette, and it certainly wouldn't be the last.

And then there are the darker outcomes. Every once in a while, the late-night fun takes a turn for the worse and results in destruction. I've come to work and found entire parts of a kitchen wall in pieces on the floor, the object of after hours aggression. And I can't count the number of times cooks have come to work the next day with black eyes and swollen hands. *I was in a bar . . . I woke up on a park bench . . . I don't know what happened.* And on occasion, when a cook pulls a no-show/no-call, nine times out of ten he is in jail.

I was older now, farther along in my career as a pastry chef, and I never worked nights anymore, which meant I was no longer witness to the after hour antics. Instead, I was told about them. *Truffle Boy had his balls out* again *last night. He chased the new sommelier around the restaurant.* I heard about the sweet-faced bartender who apparently, according to one of the cooks, "likes it rough": *She really made me grab her, hard!* I got the dish about the two coworkers who competed to take advantage of an alcoholically impaired female coworker: *You should have seen them, Doll— like two little dogs fighting for the same prize.* I found out the day after that two waiters had gotten topless on the bar—*You know how they both like to show their tits*—and what started out as flirtatious dirty dancing somehow turned sour until finally one ended up with a broken glass in her hand and the other got stitches in the emergency room. Another time, I found out that my scale had been used to parcel out a large delivery of marijuana. Whatever the story, no matter how outlandish, how unbelievable, how sick, I knew from my own earlier years that the bulk of it was probably true. There was no need to exaggerate.

When stories started trickling in about what had happened the night before that had resulted in torn-out hair and broken tables, everyone was interested in how far the limits had been pushed and who was involved this time. Some said they saw Chatos in the bar next door, missing a shoe, one eye already swelling, claiming that Will (a waiter) was trying to kill him. Will didn't say much and instead let his swollen hand and cut face speak for themselves. Chatos did, indeed, have a clump of hair missing as well as bite marks on his arm. Yes, bite marks. But that's all we ever found out. Nothing definitive. Even Paco, the dishwasher—the one other person who saw it all—kept mum. And when we asked Chatos directly *What really happened?* his answer was always the same: *The first rule about Fight Club is we don't talk about Fight Club.*

Fight Club became the stuff of legend, the subject of jokes, a day remembered fondly if not in detail. It raised the bar of what could possibly go wrong after hours and what would be acceptable. When we heard that another restaurant's late-night sexcapades, caught on videotape, had made the papers, the waiters and cooks scoffed competitively, *They got nothing on us!* And what about the two female waiters writhing topless on the bar with the broken glass? Cat-Fight Club, of course.

✦

TWENTY-SIX

(Dysfunctional) Family Meal

S he's gonna *love* this," Culo said with sadistic glee.

He and Carter were huddled by the stove, standing over a *rondeau*. Culo reached across to his station and grabbed a fistful of soft butter with his bare hand and threw it into the large pot of linguine that was already swimming in cream.

"What are you guys doing?" I asked, trying to keep the suspicion out of my voice. I knew what they were doing: They were preparing a family meal. Carter was working the hot appetizer station, which meant he was responsible for cooking the staff meal that had to be ready by four o'clock every day. But they were up to something. I could tell. No one got that excited about family meal.

Culo and Carter looked at each other, clearly struggling with whether or not they should tell me what was going on. It was a common struggle. I was one of them, part of the kitchen's inner circle (the immediate family, we called it), but they didn't always trust me. I was the pastry chef, older than all the cooks by at least eight years, and I was a woman, the only woman in the kitchen, all of which made me suspect. I was like a disapproving stepmother. It didn't help that I occasionally (and futilely) tried to be the voice of reason when their hijinks spun out of control. Despite all of this, they had just as much trouble not telling me, self-satisfied boys that they were. They couldn't help themselves, really.

"Operation Foie Gras," Carter finally said.

"Operation Foie Gras," Culo said again. "We're trying to make Adrienne fat."

I didn't get it. I thought Adrienne was one of our better waiters. She wasn't particularly friendly with the kitchen, but she was an adult and did a good job.

"She's such a slob during family meal," Culo went on. "She wants to act like a pig, then we're going to treat her like one. Fatten her up!"

"Yeah!" chimed in Carter. "Like the pig that she is!" He oinked.

"How long has Operation Foie Gras been in effect?" I asked, hiding my appall. I didn't want to alienate them and thus be deprived of information.

"Oh, about a week now, right, Carter?" said Culo.

"Yeah," said Carter. "And it's already working! Did you see her dimply ass today? She's squeezed into those pants like a sausage. She's definitely gaining weight."

"That's pretty harsh," I said.

"Dalia," urged Culo with exasperation, "have you ever watched Adrienne eat? It's disgusting. She'll just stick her fork right into the communal pot of food and eat while standing there. Do you know how disgusting that is?"

I didn't say anything; my face was blank. He went on.

"You know how when you eat spaghetti, some of it always hangs off the fork and so you bite it and let some fall back onto your plate?" he asked, not waiting for my answer. "Adrienne does that over the family pot!" He started mimicking her, snorting, while shoveling imaginary food into his mouth. I instantly got an unfortunate image of creamy pasta dripping off of Culo's goatee.

"She just shoves it in, feeding her face, letting food fall from her filthy mouth back into the communal pot that *I* have to eat out of." He was angry, defensive of any disapproval or judgment he might sense from me.

Over the years I had worked with plenty of people whom I wouldn't exactly have called friends, but Culo was the first co-worker I actually found distasteful. For the most part we got along. He was the sous-chef, and though I didn't respect him, I tried to at least respect his position as sous-chef. We got along well at first, even joked around a bit about our polarized views of the world. But over time, after listening to more and more of the crap that came out of his mouth (about women, artists, various ethnic groups, liberals, New Yorkers, anyone not like him, really), I grew to dislike him. He was the kind of loudmouth not really interested in talking or even debating. He thought that the louder his own voice, the more correct he was.

"Does Chatos know about Operation Foie Gras?" I asked, knowing that he probably did. Chatos was as bad as the rest of them.

"Yes," answered Culo, "and he loves it!"

Of course he did.

"Here," interrupted The Sherminator, another cook. Though not as inherently mean-natured as some of the other guys, it was like *Lord of the Flies* in that kitchen: prey on the weak and follow the leader, who was, unfortunately, Culo. He poured a pan full of freshly cooked diced bacon, grease and all, into the already fat-laden pasta.

"Nice!" The Sherminator said in a Borat voice. "I like!"

"Delicious!" Carter announced, testing a bite. "Like it smells!"

"So," I asked innocently, "everyone suffers because you guys hate Adrienne?"

"Everyone" really meant all the waiters, since cooks can usually, within reason, dip into their own *mise-en-place* when they want a snack. They can fry up an egg, sauté some spinach. Plus, they would spend the night sweating over a stove. What did they care if family meal was a grease-laden bowl of starch and cheese? They might as well have been preparing for a marathon.

"Fuck 'em," said Culo, the ringleader.

"Yeah," agreed Carter. "Fuck 'em."

I shrugged, grabbed an olive roll, and went back downstairs to my pastry area, leaving them to their high fives and backslapping.

It wasn't all that surprising that things could get that bad, really, at least not to me. Some people fall for the romanticized version of family meal that has been the subject of cookbooks: The entire restaurant staff sits down together at a single table to enjoy a leisurely meal that has been prepared with fresh, carefully chosen ingredients, crafted with love, and served on fine china amidst celebratory nods of shared enjoyment. But I knew better. Over my twelve years of cooking professionally, I could count on one hand the number of family meals that bore any resemblance to this idealized, truly familial rendering and still have fingers left over. Most of the time, family meal is at best an afterthought with severely limited resources.

Every day, a low- to mid-level cook who has been given the unwelcome responsibility of making the family meal will have to find something to prepare. He'll start off by spending a few minutes in the walk-in refrigerator staring at the shelves, searching for some approximation of protein. If he's lucky, he'll find five pounds of ground beef set aside, a jackpot ingredient that can be transformed into chili, Bolognese, meat loaf, meatballs, tacos, etc. But it's just as likely that he won't be so lucky, because while some restaurants do order cheap meats for the family (ground beef, pork butt, Italian sausage), there is no guarantee. Instead, maybe the cook will find something that is no longer fresh enough to be served to customers, some fish that is starting to stink but that will, once overcooked with plenty of herbs, olive oil, and lemon juice, seem perfectly acceptable to the family, especially the unwitting waiters. Or what about some charred scraps of veal breast that have already been roasted and then simmered for six hours to make sauce? Under different circumstances this meat, now completely devoid of any flavor or tenderness, would be discarded. But technically it *is* still meat that can masquerade as the foundation for family meal.

Next, this cook might look for vegetables—onions, red pepper scraps, celery, carrots—the cheap ones. Nine times out of ten he will open a can of tomatoes. Then, he will decide on the final and simplest part of the meal: the starch. Every family meal—every single one—includes a large dose of pasta, rice, polenta, or potatoes. If by chance salad greens make it to the family, you can bet they will be on their way out, wilted and slimy edged—still my biggest pet peeve. Once tossed with vinaigrette, though, the slime won't be that noticeable.

This is not to say that family meal *can't* be tasty; it can be, under the right circumstances. Some of the best Mexican food I've ever had anywhere (including Mexico) has been the product of family meal. Cooks who make trips back home often return with spices or other ingredients unavailable in New York that they share with the family, even if it's with just the immediate family: cooks, *not* waiters. I've also had amazing Greek pastitsio, Italian chicken soup, and Texas barbecue for family meal, thanks to the varied ethnic backgrounds of those who end up working in kitchens. But for every tasty soup there are many more trays of broiled fish heads, each one staring aimlessly in a different direction. For every authentic pastitsio, ten pots of pasta primavera—minus the primavera. And even when family meal tastes good, it doesn't mean we're all going to sit down together and enjoy it in a relaxing, civilized manner. Restaurant families are far too dysfunctional for that.

And in no way does the caliber of family meal directly reflect the caliber of the restaurant itself. At La Côte Basque, we had rabbit kidneys at least once a week. The slight scent of urine wafting off the hot stew prompted a common response from unsuspecting newcomers: *These mushrooms taste weird.*

So why is it that cooks who presumably have an interest and talent in preparing tasty food often put so little effort into it? Why not attack family meal as if it were a challenge on *Top Chef,* the only food show on television that garners even a modicum of respect from cooks? They don't start out apathetic. At least I didn't. When I was a new cook and given the responsibility of family meal, I felt an unspoken pressure to prove myself to my peers. Yes, making family meal can be a real pain in the ass, a chore that eats up time that can be better spent on the *real* preparation necessary for service. But somewhere in the back of my head I wondered if it was all part of a test. So, I did my best to pull something together, despite my limited time and resources. I took pride in family meal. And then, when my food was ready, the waiters would line up. Half of them, upon eyeing what I had made, would immediately leave and find food from somewhere else. The other half would stick around.

"What's this?" one of them would whine, mindlessly stirring the pot.

"Does this have any meat in it?" another would ask indignantly. "Because I don't eat meat."

"Gotta love having pasta," grumbled another thanklessly. "*Every* day."

Over time and through conversations with my more experienced fellow cooks, I came to realize that it wasn't personal. *They're just frustrated artists. Miserable fucks 'cause they have to be here waiting tables rather than doing what they really want.* It wasn't long before I easily fed into this ideology: *Fuck 'em. They'll eat what I make, and they'll like it.*

Pastry people (fair or not) never have to make family meal unless they expressly choose to. The smart pastry chef never chooses to as there are only two possible outcomes. If the meal is a success, the cooks will resent it and undercut that success: *I could make a good family meal, too, if I had that much time.* Or, should a pastry chef's family meal not succeed, the cooks will tear it apart with great satisfaction and lose even more respect for the pastry chef, who, in their minds, has an easier job as it is. My family meal responsibilities came to an abrupt end once I made the switch to working pastry full-time, and so the seed of resentment planted in me during my early years never fully blossomed. Still, I try not to get involved with family meal: I don't complain and I don't offer to help.

It's easy for cooks to feel like cogs in a wheel, one that is often churned by a demanding chef for long, hot hours, yielding little monetary reward. Add ungrateful, whining waiters to this grind, and you have a recipe for disaster. When cooks finally have the chance to feel superior, to wield what little power they have in the form of family meal, they take the chance. And they take it out on waiters.

Sometimes it's passive-aggressive. A cook might go out of his way to make something delicious, only to purposefully keep it from the waiters and share it only with the other cooks. Sometimes it's more overtly aggressive. Charlotte, the daytime sous-chef at Tonic (the sadism is by no means limited to the males), always had family meal ready and waiting for the cooks but would intentionally withhold serving utensils from the staff, just so she could gleefully watch them stare helplessly at the cooling food. She would deride any waiter who dared pop his head into the kitchen before the appointed time, sniffing for family meal: *Are you stupid? What did I say? Not until four o'clock.* Other times, she would go out of her way to make an outstanding meal and then lord over it, attacking anyone who didn't partake—*Stupid waiters, they don't know what's good*—or punishing those who didn't give her the appreciation she felt was due her—*Why do I waste my time?* Of course, no amount of thanks or appreciation would ever have satisfied her. It was the power that she craved, not the thanks.

But why do cooks really treat waiters this way? Why do they hate them? Mostly because cooks think waiters are lazy: *Do you believe that lazy bitch? She won't even walk downstairs to get some chocolate truffles for her VIP table.* Or because waiters whine about bad tips in front of cooks, knowing full well that even on the worst nights they make far more money than the cooks do: *They have no idea how easy they have it, fucking waiters.* Because they are selfish: *Look at him, picking out all the pieces of meat from the pasta. Selfish prick.* Because they are vegetarians (gasp!), artists (no!), or, what was especially appalling to Culo, liberals (the horror!). The only waiters who have half a chance are the cute ones (most cooks are still boys, after all, and suckers for a pretty face), and the few who happen to behave exactly how cooks think a waiter should, which entails a fair amount of ass kissing. Cooks don't need a reason to hate waiters, that they are waiters is reason enough. As one chef friend put it, *Waiters only care about three things: When can I leave? How much money did I make? What's for dinner?* Every misstep, every offhand comment, fuels the fire of the cooks. They hate waiters because they can. Adrienne was entrenched in a losing battle, and there was nothing she or I could do about it.

When I went back up to the kitchen, family meal was in full swing. Culo and Carter, waiting for Adrienne to arrive, had knowing grins on their faces. Carter nudged me and nodded at his cutting board.

"I made pork-skin pizza," he explained. "I took the skin from the pork belly and roasted it until it got really crispy. Then I loaded it with melted cheese and lardons, and drizzled it with chorizo oil. I put the little herb salad on top just to throw them off." He winked.

"Operation Foie Gras?" I asked.

"You know it!" he cried. I shouldn't have smiled, but I couldn't help it.

✦

TWENTY-SEVEN

Just Desserts

I can't get enough of these nuts!" Chatos said, grabbing a handful of the bee pollen almonds I'd made that morning.

I fried the sliced almonds and then, when they were still warm, tossed them in sugar, salt, and finely ground bee pollen. Along with fresh raspberries, the almonds were the garnish on my newest dessert: bamboo honey panna cotta, a dessert I was especially proud of. After years at the same job, sometimes it's easy to get stuck in a rut and simply make the same desserts over and over. And while the customers might not ever notice that the menu had stalled or know that I'd been serving the warm banana tart Tatin for more than seven years in different restaurants, I certainly did. Whenever I felt myself slacking off, I forced myself to think outside the recipe box.

Three times a week I walked through the Union Square farmer's market looking for inspiration. Fresh fruits—colorful, flavorful, and versatile—were my favorite ingredients to work with. I waited all winter and spring for the summer fruits to arrive so that finally I could make more fruit desserts. Of course, these days, we can have almost any fruit any time of the year flown in, but that doesn't mean that we should. Locally grown fruits (and vegetables, for that matter) are almost always better than anything flown in (with tropical fruits being the exception).

It was at the farmer's market that I bought the incredibly strong-flavored grade B maple syrup for the maple crème caramel I had on my menu all winter long. The simple dessert (served only with some candied pecans and sour cherry sauce) was so popular that I bought the syrup by the gallon nearly once a week.

Around the corner from the Vermont Maple Company stand was the honey guy, who had up to eight different kinds of honey, my favorite being the bamboo. The actual flower that the bees used for this honey was a Japanese ragweed, but the honey guy didn't think that sounded too appetizing and wisely named his honey after the better known botanical that it resembled: bamboo. The bamboo honey was dark and strong and complex, with definite butterscotch overtones. Perfect, I thought, for a dessert.

To showcase the honey I decided on one of the simplest desserts on the planet: panna cotta, a simple mixture of cream, gelatin, and sugar, which in this case I replaced with bamboo honey. After a single test I had my recipe. It used to take me endless trials to achieve the perfect flavor, chemistry, and texture. Now, after years of practice, it rarely takes me more than two tries.

I loved my bamboo panna cotta, but it was sweet, right on the edge of being too sweet, which, for me, could be a problem, since overly sweet desserts were my biggest pet peeve. In fact, when diners complimented me for my desserts, they often used the phrase . . . *and it's not too sweet!*

I countered the sweetness of the honey with raspberry sauce that I kept just a touch on the sour side. The acidity of the raspberries helped cut the honey, too. Finally, the bee pollen. Sliced almonds alone added textural contrast, but the bee pollen, a bright yellow dust with a floral earthiness, gave the dessert an added edge, a personal touch that made the dessert special: You would not find it just anywhere. I loved my new dessert, and I was especially glad that Chatos liked the almonds, since they were a little bit unusual and therefore a possible risk.

"Yeah," I said to him, "they turned out pretty good. I was worried that the bee pollen might absorb moisture or something and they'd get soggy, but it worked out."

"Thank God," he countered, ignoring my attempt at normal conversation. "Nobody likes soggy nuts." He grinned. I shook my head. After two years of working with Chatos, I should have expected as much.

"So, Dalia." It was Culo, casually walking over to my station.

"Yeah?" I said, looking up from my cutting board.

"You gonna help me out with my new restaurant?" he asked.

In a few weeks he'd be moving back home to open his own place. He'd talked about hiring some of the other Veritas employees as consultants for both wine and service, but I couldn't imagine he'd want me to do the same. Though we had been getting along better lately, I couldn't forget (or forgive) any of the times in the past that he'd bad-mouthed my desserts to the cooks, declaring that they were not "three-star material," as though he were an authority (Veritas was his first three-star restaurant in New York City and my third), or ridiculously charged that I used crème anglaise on too many plates, as if he knew the difference. He had even eighty-sixed a dessert for the entire night because a single customer was unhappy with it. The other cooks told me they thought the tartes Tatins were fine, and I was convinced he was simply trying to get under my skin or intimidate me. To top it off, he threw out the entire tray of Tatins, dumping hours' worth of work into the garbage and effectively destroying any evidence.

"What do you mean?" I asked innocently.

"You know, help me out with some recipes for desserts," he explained. He was smiling, like we were buddies.

I helped out people all the time with techniques, recipes, and ideas. Joey still called me from time to time for help with his menu or with some sort of pastry emergency, as did Barton. But those people were my friends. I was happy to help them out, and I knew they'd do the same for me. Culo was not my friend. I'd had to work with him for more than two years, tolerating his nasty comments, standing by while he insulted me on nearly every level. For two years, I'd had little in the way of recourse and could find no way of upsetting him the way he'd upset me. My only consolation had been the constant barrage of "Culo is gay" comments he'd had to endure. (And Chatos had no intention of ending the torment: He planned to bombard Culo's new restaurant with subscriptions to gay porn magazines taken out in Culo's name.) I couldn't believe that Culo thought I was just going to give him recipes for his restaurant, recipes that I'd worked hard on, that contributed to my reputation as a pastry chef—the only thing I really had.

"So," I asked him, choosing my words carefully, "you think that after all the times you bad-mouthed my desserts behind my back I'm going to *help* you? Just hand over recipes I've spent years working on?"

He looked stunned and held up his hands in mock surrender.

"I never bad-mouthed your desserts!" he said, his eyebrows lifted, his mouth agape.

"Come on," I said, my head cocked to the side. "We both know that's not true." My assistant, Peter, as well as the cooks with whom he'd worn out his welcome, had been more than happy to rat him out. I couldn't help smiling a tiny bit.

Culo turned away shaking his head angrily, muttering under his breath, and I went back to finishing up the rest of my work.

Culo spent the rest of the afternoon ranting well within my earshot about how all women are cunts, and though he didn't mention me by name, I knew he was talking about me, and I knew his bellowing was for the benefit of my ears. I had finally gotten under his skin, and all I'd had to do was dangle my recipes— my hard work, my ability—just out of his reach. Culo could yell all he wanted.

I couldn't fault Culo for being such a loudmouth—he was just being who he was and maybe trying to make up for what he wasn't. And I certainly couldn't blame the kitchen environment, because the very same lack of rules that allowed Culo to run his mouth and insult everyone also allowed me to brazenly call him an asshole from time to time or ignore him altogether. Kitchen law demands that cooks blindly obey their chef like unquestioning recruits, but as long as the food gets made the way the boss demands, there is enormous personal freedom. Over the years I've tolerated lots of hard work, long hours, and the occasional unpleasant coworker, but I have never, ever had to compromise who I am.

More than once I've compared my life in the kitchen to that of my office life so many years ago. I imagine the president of the company roaming the halls yelling that the vice president of sales and marketing is gay—although the odds of that actually happening are very slim to none, given the fact that there are now laws preventing that kind of behavior. But had I remained there, I would have had to expend lots of energy on superficial things like my personal appearance, small talk, and office politics—things for which I have no natural knack—to advance. Instead, freed from these kinds of distractions, I've been able to focus on the work at hand—the craft—that I really love.

But as I grow older I cannot deny that my place in the restaurant world may have to change. As turning forty comes closer, it becomes more difficult to imagine a future spent in front of the oven of a high-end restaurant. And while the restaurant world may be slowly (very slowly) evolving into a slightly less antagonistic arena, kitchens largely remain unfriendly places for anyone unwilling to fully dedicate the entirety of their lives to the job.

It is only in hindsight that I can truly realize how lucky I've been to have worked with chefs like Joey, who not only taught me how to be a good cook and an even better pastry chef but also never once gave me cause to think that I was any less qualified for my job simply for being a woman. On the contrary, he was not shy about pointing out what he saw as the advantages of working with women. Thanks to chefs like him and all the wonderfully talented women I've worked with, I've been able to ignore the sexist comments and managed to work through the fears and failures. I can now look forward in my career without second-guessing my abilities or my place in the kitchen. But with age comes a slow shift in priorities that for me includes having a child.

With all of the experience and knowledge I've gained, I know better than anyone that if kitchens can sometimes be unfriendly places for women, they can be downright dangerous for a pregnant woman. There are the obvious hazards for a pregnant woman (the long days spent entirely on her feet, the heavy lifting), which are nearly impossible to avoid despite the well-meaning but misguided suggestions from innocent outsiders, like bringing in a stool on which to work or simply asking someone else to take care of all the lifting. There are less obvious obstacles. I've heard of one pastry chef who had to quit her job early on simply because her severe morning sickness made her retch at the first breath of the kitchen smells. And never mind the slew of regular doctor's appointments. You can't just take two hours out of a restaurant workday. An extended maternity leave might seem like a logical answer, except that in businesses with fewer than fifty employees (i.e., lots of small restaurants) maternity leave is a lucky extravagance rather than a legal mandate.

Of course chefs and pastry chefs do have children, but in my experience it requires a well-paid and supportive partner or family so that she can take off the time she needs. And what about returning to work? Most pastry chef salaries hardly allow for full-time caregivers, especially when full time for us is in excess of forty hours a week. And as much as the determined, resolute woman inside of me believes it can be done, even I have a difficult time imagining myself slipping away to the filthy restroom for half-hour breaks every day to pump breast milk. And should I have to call in sick one day because my infant is ill, who will make the desserts? In small restaurants of precisely the type I have worked in over the recent years, the answer would mostly likely be: no one.

Despite all this, after twelve years, I still love cooking, still love making desserts, still love even simple tasks like peeling apples. I love the joy that comes with knowing that something I made brought a smile and maybe even sincere pleasure to people, and I love that slices of warm, freshly baked brioche can quiet a kitchen full of foulmouthed cooks. The novelty of finding a new restaurant, discovering a new taste or a fresh way of mixing flavors remains endlessly invigorating, and food is still the most exhilarating part of any trip: to my mother's farm in Tennessee, to the Sinai Desert, even just to another borough. For now, at least, I'll continue cooking and baking and feeding people in some shape or form, providing the most basic of needs and the simplest of pleasures. And shallow though it may be, I will always love the rote question *And what do you do?* because I know I'll get a look of surprised delight in people's eyes when I tell them that I am a pastry chef.

Acknowledgments

Many sincere thanks to—

My editor, Peternelle van Arsdale, and my agent, Kirsten Neuhaus, for believing I could write this book in the first place.

Everyone at Putnam for their overwhelming support of *Spiced*, but especially Ivan Held, Kate Stark, Marilyn Ducksworth, Mih-Ho Cha, Lisa Amoroso, Dick Heffernan and the entire sales force, and Rachel Holtzman.

Sarah Shatz, photographer extraordinaire, Mary Jones, and Gail Schoenberg.

The very accommodating Restaurant Jean Claude and everyone at Dressler restaurant, especially Polo Dobkin and Colin Devlin.

All the cooks and chefs I've worked with who have made my life infinitely richer, but especially Scott Bryan, Scott Barton, and most of all, Joseph Fortunato.

Janah and Lara Feldman, for their lifetime of support and friendship.

And finally, my parents, brother, and extended family, without whom I would not be who I am today.